Moshe Rashkes • Doomed to Glory

Moshe Rashkes

DOOMED TO GLORY

Translated by Mali Ohana

MILO PUBLISHING HOUSE LTD.

Cover Design: Shuki Dochovni
Cover Photograph: Oren Agmon

ISBN 978-965-405-014-2

In memory of my mother, Golda

CONTENTS

III - REAL SPORTS HEROES

IV – IN THE PATHS OF BENEVOLENCE

I
BACK TO LIFE

A BATTLE FOR IMAGE

Society's attitude towards the disabled has a long history. For generations, the disabled were rejected, and were regarded as being feeble and insignificant. Quite often, they were seen as beggars parading their disabilities to demonstrate their helplessness in order to arouse pity and provide for their own subsistence.

The twentieth century brought some change. It would be a mistake, however, to assume that this trend derived from a positive development or any improvement in human nature. The process was rooted in more practical considerations. The two world wars left millions of disabled veterans, who were thrown back into society with a promise of moral and financial restitution. At the same time, as a result of improved technology and medical services, there was a substantial decrease in the mortality rates of those born with congenital abnormalities. Those who had once been foredoomed to death now stood a good chance of survival – as disabled individuals. The size of the world's disabled population increased in the twentieth century. It was still a minority, but its size could no longer be ignored.

In antiquity, the unyielding, militaristic Spartans killed their weak and feeble on the pretext that they were a burden on the state. In the modern welfare state, however, most believed that such a solution could not be tolerated by the human mindset and moral values. The whole world nevertheless bore witness to the barbaric Nazi regime, which proved otherwise. The Nazis initially took action against the most helpless and weak stratum of society – the physically and mentally disabled – denying their very right to exist. The Nazis segregated their disabled victims in concentration camps, where they were victims of an experimental extermination process, cloaked in the misleadingly euphemistic term "Euthanasia"– or "mercy killing". In the course of this process, the Nazis murdered tens of thousands of German nationals who were ill or disabled, including even their own seriously disabled war veterans. This experiment was the basis for a well-organized, state-of-the-art World War II killing machine, which murdered those who had no right to exist in the eyes of the state – and this mainly meant the Jews.

The defeat of Nazi Germany led to a considerable

increase in the population of war disabled. These disabled individuals gradually gained a recognition of their own worth that had been lacking in previous generations; they were no longer willing to bear the label of welfare-recipients. To ensure that the state paid its dues to its war injured, these war veterans began to organize and join forces. The recognition achieved by the disabled war veterans' organizations in the various countries motivated the civilian disabled to follow in their footsteps. Thus were created the foundations and public setting that enabled the disabled to defend and even expand the rights to which they were entitled.

As public recognition of the disabled increased, a way was sought to enable them to discard the label of helplessness that had been hung around their necks since time immemorial. This was the global backdrop for the birth of disabled sports, inspired by Professor Ludwig Guttman. Among the challenges and aspirations experienced by the disabled participating in sports activities was also the basic right to enjoy sports and, through this activity, to gain mental relief, sports achievements and social prominence. Society denied this right to the disabled in a way that was both condescending and overly considerate: "there's no way you can do it". It was precisely this perception, which unintentionally deprived the disabled of rights that inalienably belonged to all non-disabled, which fired the disabled with motivation.

The discharge and return home of hundreds of thousands of disabled soldiers from the battlefields of

World War II prompted the first important steps taken by disability sports on an international scale. The harsh lessons of war spurred many ex-servicemen, of all nationalities, to become involved in working towards a better future – mainly in the area of rehabilitation of injured war veterans. Thus, in 1951, the World War Veterans' Federation was founded on the initiative of Americans Elliot Newcomb and Norman Hector. This body accrued fame and prestige in the 1950s. By the early 1960s, however, it was already clear that these discharged soldiers had not become a real political force. The World War Veterans' Federation did make important achievements in promoting legislation in Europe, the United States, and, particularly, in the underdeveloped countries. One of the practical issues in which the Federation was involved was the development and promotion of rehabilitative sports activities for war disabled. Israel was one of the first countries to take part in this campaign.

THE MIRACLE WORKER
FROM STOKE MANDEVILLE

The atomic bomb detonated on Hiroshima and Nagasaki towards the end of World War II exposed the absolute horror of such all-out war. It was almost impossible to ascertain the precise number of casualties. In addition to loss of life and bereavement, the war resulted in tens of millions of human beings with physical injuries. It is difficult to judge which type of disability is the hardest to bear. Many consider paraplegia – total paralysis – to be the most devastating for the human body and mind. The sight of wounded soldiers in military hospitals, paralysed from the waist down and dying in agony, was a common experience of World War II. These harsh scenes reinforced the approach formulated in British medical circles, that paraplegia was an irreversible physical calamity.

For this reason, the appointment of a new director of the Spinal Cord Unit at Stoke Mandeville Hospital, near London, was of crucial importance to the war victims. Hundreds of paralysed British ex-servicemen were concentrated there, together with civilians who had been injured in the barbaric Luftwaffe air raids. A Jewish refugee doctor, Ludwig Guttman, a short, thickset figure in his mid-forties, whose face was almost always wreathed in an abashed smile, had been chosen for the task. In Germany, Dr. (later Prof. Sir) Ludwig Guttman had been a renowned neurosurgeon who developed new methods of treatment for paraplegics. This hadn't helped him escape the long arm of the Nazi regime. Like other Jewish doctors and scientists, Guttman fled to Great Britain with his family, where he now worked in a clinic for a modest annual salary. The decision to appoint Guttman was undoubtedly influenced by his innovative methods. The British health authorities felt that they had nothing to lose in their choice of Dr. Guttman. The paralysed were considered to be a lost case anyway, and it was better to choose a doctor who was still able to give some hope.

Guttman's childhood in Germany had passed uneventfully, apart from one anti-Semitic incident at school when an upset Aryan pupil had called one of his Jewish classmates a "dirty Jew". Young and hot-headed, Guttman had punched the culprit. Even as a youngster, he fought for justice. Although Ludwig played football and took part in track events, his physical appearance seemed to epitomize the anti-Semitic image of the small and insignificant Jew. Guttman sought to break out of this mould by developing his physical strength. As a student, Guttman joined the German Students' Fencing Association. He hoped that his involvement in this noble activity would give him an image of courage and boldness – so different from the downtrodden Jews of Germany. But when, to his surprise, he came up against anti-Semitism in the Fencing Association, he reacted with great anger, and founded a Jewish students' fencing association. He did not, however, adopt the Zionist agenda, and regarded himself as a loyal Jewish citizen of Germany.

Guttman was still a teenager when World War I broke out in 1914. He volunteered as a medic in the mining region of Germany. Because of the cave-ins at the mines, the hospital where he served cared mainly for spinal cord injuries. Here Guttman encountered typical cases of paralysis. Despite devoted medical care, he also witnessed the swift death of a young paraplegic miner. The World War I mortality rate among spinal cord casualties in the armies of the West was high. Fifty percent of those injured died in the first few months after being wounded. The mortality rate was eighty percent for those who succeeded in surviving the first three years, usually in gloomy institutions. The paraplegics were depressed by the wretchedness of their predicament and the inability of medicine to save them. They gradually lost the will to survive.

With the outbreak of World War II, the hospitals in Britain were inundated with paralysed military personnel, battle wounded and civilians injured in the German air raids. This reality spurred the British health authorities on to establish special units caring for spinal cord injuries. The units operated alongside and in co-operation with existing hospitals in various parts of the country. When Dr. Guttman was appointed, he felt that these separate units were unable to provide the range of treatments necessary for paralysed patients. He proposed that a single hospital be assigned as a national medical centre, specializing in spinal cord injuries. The hospital he chose was the one at Stoke Mandeville.

The welcome Guttman received from the disheartened hospital staff at Stoke Mandeville, understandably, was one of misgiving and restraint. Pressure sores, caused by the rupturing of skin stretched over prominent bones from the pressure of endlessly lying in bed, are one of the most serious dangers to bedridden invalids. When the wound becomes infected, it leads to a general deterioration in the patient's physical and psychological condition. To avoid this predictable problem, Guttman instructed his staff to re-position his patients every two hours. This reduced the pressure on the patients' wounds by half. At first, the staff regarded this treatment with doubt and frustration; for them it seemed like a lot of additional hard work – to no avail. Guttman began making surprise inspections, during the day and also at night, to ensure that his instructions were being carried out. After a short time, it became clear that there was indeed an improvement in the condition of his patients.

Guttman dedicated part of his time to reading his patients' diaries. They described the trauma of paraplegia, their relationships with their families and friends – and particularly with their girlfriends. He was stirred by his patients' desire for movement, and encouraged them to develop games they could play in their wheelchairs. They used crutches and sticks as bats and a ball made out of a bundle of rags. Guttman realized the magic power and attraction of the ball. He observed the alertness and momentum that accompanied the game, which caused the disabled individual engaged in sport to behave as an ordinary, healthy person. The ambition, initiative, physical and emotional strength, and sometimes even the aggressive behaviour, developed and grew stronger. No medicine or treatment could generate such an awakening.

Guttman very quickly learned the potential of sports, which – in his eyes – was a vital form of treatment. It was, moreover, willingly and enthusiastically accepted by his patients. The sports activities made a very positive difference to their state of mind. His patients started to show an increased interest in the sports pages of the newspapers. It was now time to develop a new game for wheelchairs – basketball. This game provides physical and mental challenges, and teaches its participants how to work as a team. Guttman observed that sports activity developed the muscles of the upper body. It also strengthened the respiratory musculature, weakened by prolonged inaction. But the most important contribution was emotional. The paraplegic, whose fate seemed to have been sealed, began to regain self-confidence. He became more active, and discovered a renewed interest in life. Society's attitude towards the active disabled also improved. The paralysed patients were able to tell their visitors about what they were doing, instead of complaining about what they were unable to do. This experiment led Guttman to take the innovative step of including sports activities in the Stoke Mandeville Hospital's rehabilitation programme.

Guttman, who gave the impression of being the stereotypical dry Prussian, took a warm personal interest in his patients. He discussed with them the magnificence of the muscles of the upper body, and how they could be developed even more. He seemed to find irresistible the mythological figure he portrayed, based on the Olympic ideal that had become so popular.

One of the stumbling blocks for wheelchair sport was the medical establishment's conservative and cautious attitude to this new venture, which Guttman presented as an advanced form of medical treatment. The medical establishment was concerned that the players' legs would be injured by collision with the fast-moving wheelchairs, and that such uncontrolled blows to the body would cause additional injury to the already damaged spinal cord. There was also anxiety that such energetic activity, while seated in a wheelchair, could accelerate the development of pressure sores. Even though Guttman developed methods of protecting the wheelchair rider, there were very few doctors in the world who supported his ground-breaking methods. Guttman understood the necessity for an extensive public relations campaign to win social and state recognition of his innovative venture. In his efforts, he also came up against a reluctant media. Journalists, like people all over the world, found it difficult to regard sport for the disabled as being on the same level as regular sport. This led Guttman to think about the possibility of holding international sports games for the disabled, even perhaps an Olympic Games for the disabled. As a practical man, Guttman knew that this could not be realized immediately. The way to achieve his goal would depend on deeds rather than words. In 1948, the year that the State of Israel was established, he organized the first sports games for the disabled in Stoke Mandeville, seeing this as a first step in his long pursuit of international recognition.

Although only sixteen disabled individuals from England took part in these first games, Guttman believed that they could become an international event. His expectations were partially realized in 1949, when some sixty athletes from Great Britain took part in the games. In 1952 the games became semi-international, and the total number of participants reached 130, including a very small Israeli delegation. But the year that truly made its mark internationally was 1953, with 200 competitors, from Great Britain, The Netherlands,

France, Finland, Canada, and Israel. Guttman understood that, in order to win greater recognition, he would have to attract the support of well-known celebrities. His overtures to the British royal family were well received, mainly because the victims in question were mostly disabled British ex-servicemen, whose rehabilitation was the responsibility of the kingdom. The support of the royal family gave Dr. Guttman confidence – and also the conviction – that the movement he had founded was on the right path.

THE HUMAN COST

Five Arab states* attacked Israel in 1948 in order to prevent the implementation of the United Nations' partition plan. This plan divided the ancient Land of Israel, formerly under British mandate, into two states, one Jewish and one Arab. Like all wars, the human cost was devastating – and painful for all involved.

***

It was difficult to breathe in the clammy and dust-filled air. The heavy machine-gun bullets struck the

---

* The attacking states were: Egypt, Jordan, Iraq, Syria, Lebanon and the Palestinian Arab forces.

armoured plating, threatening to blow it to smithereens. The armoured vehicle in which Private Michael Ben-Naftali huddled was under heavy fire from the Arab Legion. Ben-Naftali crouched over the antiquated Lewis Gun, and returned fire through the firing loopholes. Suddenly, one of the soldiers, in a dazed state of shock, crawled towards the closed door in an attempt to escape from the cramped space. He barely managed to get the door open a crack before another soldier pulled it shut. In that brief moment, a burst of machine-gun fire penetrated the AFV and Ben-Naftali was hit. He felt a massive blow to the lower part of his body. His heart beat wildly and a terrible fear took control over him. "Oh God, have those bullets cut my body in half?" he wondered. His fingers felt a hot unyielding lump where he had been wounded. He couldn't feel anything when he pinched it. He raised his hands – they were covered in blood.

Ben-Naftali tried to control his fear, and persuade himself that the numbness would pass. He heard a terrifying buzzing in his ears, and couldn't breathe. A tremendous exhaustion weighed him down, and he was completely unable to move. All he wanted to do was sleep. Maybe then he would wake up, and discover it had passed. A medic bent over him, and tried to prevent him from falling asleep. The firing continued. His ears became the focal point of his existence, magnifying everything he heard around him. And then, abruptly, there was silence. He heard only the faint mumbling of the medic in his ears, like a rising and falling, stuttering echo, repeating again and again: "Everything... will... be... okay".

When he woke up, he became aware of intense flashing lights. They shone directly at him out of the fog in front of his face. It was as though lighted matches were being poked into his eyes. He tried to shift position – but couldn't. A constant humming rang in his ears, accompanied by a thumping sound. He gradually realized that this was the sound of his heart. He heard a female voice and, when he saw the white-uniformed nurse by his side, understood that he was in hospital. When he regained consciousness some hours later, he became aware of bottles of fluids hanging over his head and a metal canopy covering a large part of his body. He continued breathing stertorously though a parched throat. After a while, a blurry blonde-haired figure bent over the side of the bed. She stroked his head and murmured "Mishka... Mishka...", the special nickname his mother always called him. From that time on, his mother was constantly by his side, wiping his brow and helping him to drink.

Some days later, when Ben-Naftali was feeling a little better, his mother tried to persuade him to eat some broth. She had great faith in the healing powers of food and water. The doctors gradually made it clear to her, however, that her son was paralysed or – in medical terms – a paraplegic. He was one of the first residents of Pavilion 19 at Tel Hashomer Hospital. There were a dozen or so fellow ex-servicemen who shared his fate in this large ward. All the patients were bedridden, and attached to various tubes that entered and exited their bodies. The doctors, nurses and staff walked around quietly and sombrely, cut off from the outside world and everything that was happening in the newborn State.

Meanwhile, Israel's heroic struggle against the invading Arab armies continued and even intensified. The young state now also found itself having to deal with the complex problems of providing medical treatment for some six thousand war disabled, including bilateral-limb amputees, visually-impaired, and paraplegics like Ben-Naftali. The prime minister and minister of defence, David Ben Gurion, determined that the care of the war disabled would be under the auspices of the Ministry of Defence. But this measure did not solve the practical problems of caring for the disabled in a newborn state, already inundated with complicated problems of economy and absorption of refugee immigrants from the European holocaust. The Israel War Veterans' Organization, later to be called Zahal Disabled Veterans Organization, was established against this backdrop. One of the first steps taken by the Organization was to liaise directly with Ben-Gurion. But, apart from agreeing that the paraplegics should be concentrated in one medical care unit, on the British model, a solution to the paraplegics' medical and psychological problems was hard to find.

Pavilion 19 at Tel Hashomer Hospital (later to become known as the Sheba Medical Centre) was assigned as the centre for the treatment of spinal cord injuries, under the directorship of Prof. Chaim Sheba.

Sheba had served as Commander of the Medical Corps
during Israel's War of Independence. Despite the
dedicated medical treatment that Ben-Naftali and his
paralysed comrades-in-arms received, here too – as in
Stoke Mandeville – despair was the patients' main
enemy, and, it would seem, also that of their carers.
The atmosphere that prevailed in the pavilion matched
the acrid odour deriving from the over-generous use of
disinfectants, intended to subdue the unpleasant smells
coming from the patients' bodies. As time went by with
no real improvement in the medical conditions of these
patients, the mood became even gloomier.

When Prime Minister Ben-Gurion first visited
Pavilion 19 at Tel Hashomer, his apprehension was
palpable. Accompanied by Professors Chaim Sheba and
Ernst Spira, and by the department doctors, Ben-Gurion
strode slowly between the beds, around which there
was a strong smell of carbolic acid – a double dose of
which had been sprayed that morning. He lingered
beside each and every bed, and spoke with the paralysed
veterans. Sorrow was deeply etched on his features,
which became more and more lined with concern as
the tour went on. From time to time, he asked questions
of the medical entourage, and was given explanations
with a heavy German accent by Professor Spira, a
distinguished specialist. Spira also introduced each
patient, acting as a kind of MC for this unhappy event.
Ben-Gurion stayed by Ben-Naftali's bed a little longer
than was his wont, maybe because Mishka greeted him
with a big grin. Ben-Gurion returned an embarrassed

smile, and asked him the usual set of questions about
his home, his army unit and how he had been injured.

"...And the treatment here? How's the treatment
going?" Ben-Gurion tentatively enquired.

Unlike most of the other patients, Ben-Naftali
answered: "I think they're doing everything they can".

Spira seemed a little put out by the sudden personal
contact between his patient and the prime minister. He
was perhaps concerned that Ben-Naftali would
overwhelm Ben-Gurion with complaints and grievances
regarding medical matters – a subject on which the
prime minister knew little. This had happened several
times in the past. Spira turned his glance towards the
next bed, as if gently urging Ben-Gurion to conclude
his conversation. Spira began loudly giving details
about the patient lying there. Ben-Gurion, seeking to
avoid misunderstandings, apologetically murmured to
Ben-Naftali: "If there are any problems, you can always
call me". He made it obvious that he was apologising
for the fact that, despite his high standing, here he was
not entirely master of his own movements. Ben-Naftali
smiled when the prime minister moved on to the next
bed.

"What a wonderful lad... wonderful...!" Ben-Gurion
exclaimed to the medical entourage as he left Pavilion
19. "What did you say his name was?" he asked Prof.
Spira.

"Mishka", came the answer.

Ben-Gurion quickly noted the name in the little
notebook that he kept in the pocket of his army safari

shirt. After his visit to Pavilion 19, Ben-Gurion consulted with representatives of the war disabled. He wanted to know what more could be done, and how these paralysed veterans could best be rehabilitated. The reply was to seek advice from the renowned international specialist in this field, Prof. Ludwig Guttman of Stoke Mandeville. Ben-Gurion immediately sent Guttman an invitation to come to Israel as quickly as possible. Guttman was very proud of the fact that the State of Israel, so soon after its establishment and despite the heavy warfare still prevailing, was absorbing thousands of Jewish refugees from the European holocaust. He was very moved by the invitation – from the State of Israel, the Jewish homeland – which recognized his ability to help its war wounded. He would be glad to fulfil his duty as a Jew and as a doctor. He sent a positive response and, very soon after, late one evening, landed at Lod airport. The morning after his arrival, Guttman came to Pavilion 19, and spent most of the day examining the patients and discussing their cases with the medical staff.

The next day, Guttman dropped in to meet Ben-Gurion at his Tel Aviv office. As the two men sat down on the simply upholstered armchairs, Ben-Gurion shot an enquiring glance at his guest. Guttman spoke English with a heavy German accent. He explained that what was involved in most cases was a basic and irreversible injury. At the same time, he added in an encouraging tone, it was possible to improve the patients' general condition, and to strengthen those parts of the body that had not been injured. Using the reserves of the healthy parts of the body, the disabled patient could be encouraged to lead an active life. One of the means to this end was sport. Ben-Gurion held the professor's arm the whole time he was speaking, in a tangible expression of affection. When Guttman finished talking, Ben-Gurion quizzed him with a host of questions. "What more can we do? Is there a chance that future discoveries will change things?"

Guttman's responses were based on his wide experience at Stoke Mandeville. He recommended that a special effort be made to prevent and treat the pressure sores, and that more physiotherapy and occupational therapy be offered. All this was necessary so that the patients could leave hospital as quickly as possible. But, the professor emphasized, these important efforts would be to no avail if a sports programme wasn't developed. Such a programme should begin operating immediately, and should accompany the disabled for the rest of their lives. This would maximize their rehabilitation and their life expectancy. Ben-Gurion wondered how sports could be considered a medical treatment, but, sticking to his principle of almost always taking an expert's reasonable advice, he adopted Prof. Guttman's recommendations.

BEGINNINGS AT
TEL HASHOMER

The Tel Hashomer Hospital stood on a desolate spot surrounded by untended fields. It was the most suitable place available to begin the work with the IDF paraplegics. However, the response of the disabled veterans themselves was unenthusiastic. Like most other people at that time, the paraplegics found it difficult to understand how sports activities could help them. The activities were carried out at the hospital in cooperation with the Israel War Veterans' Organization, which sent emissaries to the hospital to persuade the disabled to participate. In the first six months, however, only about a dozen disabled regularly took part in these sports activities.

Thanks to a grant received from the World War Veterans' Federation, a first delegation of disabled sportsmen got organized in 1952 to take part in the Stoke Mandeville competitions at the end of July. There was great excitement and enthusiasm among the disabled at Tel Hashomer. The leading lights of the group, including Mishka Ben-Naftali, were chosen for this delegation, and the team departed for London on a Philippine Airlines plane. Lack of experience in flying paraplegics led the airline to transport them on stretchers at the rear of the plane, crammed together as closely as possible. It resembled a hastily prepared battlefield departure stage for wounded servicemen. In order not to scare the other passengers, a curtain was put up to conceal them from view. These special arrangements, in such a gloomy atmosphere, were typical of the attitude towards disabled the world over. For lack of funding, the members of the delegation travelled to London without a professional escort, which made things very difficult. Their difficulties were greatly reduced when Renee Berman, then president of WIZO in London, contacted the Israeli group, and took them under her wing. The Israeli threesome displayed great resourcefulness in face of their difficulties. They took great pride in the fact that they had been motivated to do things that they could not have dreamed of doing a year earlier. And, indeed, after this trip to Stoke Mandeville, activities and enthusiasm amongst the disabled intensified.

Rivalry over participation in the 1953 delegation also

greatly increased the competitive spirit. Towards June 1953 a group was chosen, based on attendance at training sessions and individual achievements. This time, an escort was sent with the group – Nurse Esther Feldman. On the train ride between London and Stoke Mandeville, Feldman got into conversation with an attractive Jewish woman, Eve Gertler, who lived in Aylesbury, close to Stoke Mandeville. She and her husband, David, later became friends of the Centre.

Participation in an international event and the contacts forged with disabled athletes from other countries were very exciting for the Israeli contingent. Because of the economic situation in Israel at the time, it was quite difficult to leave the country. As a result of the war, Israel was still depleted of human and financial resources. Food rationing was still in effect, and foreign currency expenditure was discouraged. Disabled sports opened a door to the outside world. This awareness encouraged the Israeli disabled athletes to recognize and realize their own potential. Sports activities had taught Ben-Naftali how important the wheelchair was to the disabled individual's mobility, and how vital it was that the wheelchair be reliable and easy to manoeuvre. The wheelchairs the disabled received from the hospital were heavy and cumbersome. Ben-Naftali was blessed with a highly developed technical bent, and he started working on blueprints for a new and reliable wheelchair.

Ben-Naftali made use of the hospital workshop to construct, with his own hands, a special sports wheelchair. Later, when he moved to the adapted house constructed for him in north Tel Aviv by the Ministry of Defence, he organized his own small workshop where he continued to build his prototype wheelchair. After a few months, it was ready for operation, and polished to a high gloss. Ben-Naftali brought his wheelchair to his training sessions at Tel Hashomer. The wheelchair was passed from one paraplegic to another. After they had finished trying it out, Ben-Naftali had more than a dozen orders in hand. He expanded his workshop and began building the wheelchairs ordered by his friends. Meanwhile, he also took part in the delegation to the Stoke Mandeville Games, where he had the opportunity to try out American, German and British wheelchairs. He resolved that his wheelchairs would comprise all the benefits to be found in these others. He enthusiastically made up a suitable name for his wheelchair – M.B.N. – the initials of his name.

The wheelchairs that Ben-Naftali built in Israel were quickly snapped up. They were lightweight and more comfortable than the wheelchairs purchased by the Ministry of Defence. It didn't take long before the Israeli Ministry of Defence began ordering wheelchairs from Ben-Naftali, who had now established a small factory in Ramat Gan. He derived great pride and satisfaction from the fact that he was creating a product that brought such benefit to friends who shared his fate.

The orders for Ben-Naftali's wheelchairs increased to such a degree that he was no longer able to meet the local demand. His wheelchairs attracted growing attention also at the Stoke Mandeville Games. Wheelchair manufacturers from all over the world took great interest in the wheelchair designed by Mishka Ben-Naftali. As the Israeli wheelchair basketball team's achievements soared in the international arena, the merits of the M.B.N. wheelchair became even more widely known.

II

NEW HOPE
FOR THE DISABLED

THE EPIDEMIC

The summer flu that scourged Israel following the cold
winter of 1950 aroused no special attention at first. The
hot sirocco winds always bring the summer diseases
with them – infections and stomach upsets. This time,
it was mainly children who fell victim – but even this
fact didn't arouse any special curiosity. Children are
always prone to mysterious maladies that usually
disappear by themselves after a day or two. The general
public went about its daily affairs, trying to avoid the
exhausting heat of the sun. The beaches and swimming
pools were crowded with tens of thousands of bathers,
who contentedly splashed around in the refreshing
water. These were the finest hours for the ice cream

and soda vendors, who cooled their wares in boxes filled to the brim with crushed ice.

However, anxiety was mounting at the Hadassah Hospital in Tel Aviv. Growing numbers of concerned parents were bringing their infants in with high temperatures and respiratory difficulties. Over the previous few years, this phenomenon had become a familiar one in Europe, America and other parts of the world. It even had a name – Poliomyelitis. Yet the doctors in Israel still hoped and prayed that the number of cases would be small, as had been the case the previous year. In medical circles, however, the question was already in the air. Was there going to be a Polio epidemic? Professional accountability denied the doctors the right to keep information to themselves. The children's parents, schools and home environments had to be cautioned against the risk of infection through poor hygiene. The general public paid little attention to the news items that appeared in the papers and on the radio about "the disease". Israelis were more concerned about the weather, the food rationing, the condition of the transit camps constructed for the incoming flow of immigrants, and, above all, the security situation in the fledgling state.

However, the whole world, and even tiny Israel, soon realized that a new, frightening era had begun. Polio struck mainly children; those who survived were left deformed and paralysed for the rest of their lives.

Preventive health measures were initiated all over the country. The Ministry of Health and local authorities soon discovered flaws in the sewage system. The repairs required time and money. While the government and local authorities tried to improve the health facilities, the general public developed its own methods of defence. They refused to accept back into their midst those children who had recovered from the disease, fearing that they would infect the others. All scientific explanations to the contrary, explaining that they had nothing to fear, were received with suspicion. People believed that the health authorities were trying to conceal the truth. A wall of fear was constructed around the young Polio victims, who were now portrayed as Public Enemy No. 1. Information on the subject of the epidemic, which had earlier been relegated to the inside pages of the newspapers, now received eye-catching headlines on the front page. Despite the oppressive heat of the summer, the beaches suddenly emptied, and the once crowded swimming pools were deserted. The public suspected that the virus was passed on through person-to-person contact in the water.

The cinemas, too, lost their audiences, especially in the afternoon hours, when parents feared that the stuffy air of the crowded cinema was conducive to the spread of the disease. The chemists, on the other hand, experienced a boom in sales. The public rediscovered the importance of washing hands with soap and water before eating, and of disinfecting fruit and vegetables. Carbolic acid, caustic substances and other disinfectants became top sellers. But the most efficient and sure preventative, in the eyes of the public, was to keep away from the ailing child and his family.

The situation was even worse in the transit camps where the new immigrants were being absorbed. Here the standards of sanitation were low. Many of the parents had only recently immigrated to Israel from the East and were very religious. Their greater fear was that if their children were taken to the hospitals they would be spirited away to a godless environment. Thus, there were large numbers of ailing children, hidden away in the tents and makeshift huts of the transit camps, without any suitable medical care.

Desperate parents sought comfort in prayer, in swearing oaths, magical spells, making donations to the synagogues and sending protestations heavenward. Blessings from the sages were considered to be an efficient remedy, and the local rabbis organized nightly gatherings of learned scholars to read verses from the Book of Psalms. Exorcisms were carried out, the devil was banished with fire and incense, and the bodies of some children were smeared with various ointments, ash and paraffin. Even the spiritual world was recruited for the battle against Polio; mediums and necromancers sought contact with the spirits, asking for their advice and assistance.

In America and Great Britain, hundreds of scientists and doctors worked diligently to find a cure for the virus causing this disease, which was no newcomer. The German Professor Jakob Heine was the first to define it, in 1840. About a hundred years later, Dr. Frank Golan, a Jewish American Polio victim, succeeded in isolating the Polio virus, thus paving the way for other doctors to develop a vaccine. Dr. Jonas Salk, an American doctor from a traditionally Jewish background, was the first to develop such a vaccine. After five long years of hard labour and frustrating experiments, Salk succeeded. Based on a virus that he had grown and clinically "killed" in the laboratory, Salk was able to give the world a vaccine against Polio. Human beings could now be injected with the vaccine. Salk refused to patent the vaccine he had discovered, and gave up the profits he could have received. Soon thereafter, Professor Albert Sabin, another American Jew, and a Zionist, developed a second vaccine. Sabin's vaccine was based on the live virus weakened under laboratory conditions, but still strong enough to reproduce only in the intestinal tract, where it developed local immunity. The weakened virus was unable to continue its route from the intestinal tract to the central nervous system. Sabin's virus was easier to administer, as the two-drop dose could be taken sublingually. To this day, these two vaccines remain the only defence against Poliomyelitis.

However, the over fourteen thousand disabled children who survived the epidemic in Israel were left with deep psychological scars, largely as a result of the public's attempts to avoid contact with them. The young victims of the epidemic found it difficult to understand such behaviour. From cuddled and loved children they had become, almost overnight, a sort of monster pariah. For this reason, the speedy physical and psychological rehabilitation of these children was considered to be of prime importance.

The Israeli medical establishment proposed that the disabled children be concentrated in special hospitals, the main one being at Assaf Harofeh near Tel Aviv. With its depleted resources, this was a national catastrophe for tiny Israel. The national conscience began to awaken. People of sensitivity felt that deserting these children and their families was a disgrace to Israeli society and the Jewish spirit. A first group of volunteers started coming to the hospitals, to extend a helping hand wherever needed. Hard work awaited the volunteers in the transit camps – to try and persuade the families to entrust their children to the hospitals.

The need for planning was vital and urgent. ILAN volunteers were swiftly organized in Tel Aviv by Betty Dubiner, Dan Piness, Shoshana Ron, Chana Laor (Sandovsky), Leah Rapaport, Shmuel Hirschfeld and Arthur Broza. Dubiner felt that the activities had so far lacked momentum, and initiated the establishment of the Polio Association. Influenced by the promotional methods used in the United States, Dubiner's group burst onto the streets in a blast of publicity. They demanded that every citizen be involved in the battle against the epidemic and the rehabilitation of its victims, either by volunteering or by making a financial contribution. Their main goal was to raise funds to purchase the vaccine in the United States, joining forces with the Ministry of Health to obtain the vaccine developed by Dr. Jonas Salk. At this time, the American government was not exporting the vaccine until immunization had been completed in America itself. However, since most of those involved in the development of the vaccine were Jews, for whom the plight of Israel's children was of special importance, the Jewish and Israeli envoys were able to purchase the vaccine. Thus, thanks to Betty Dubiner, Prof. Melnick and others, the first consignment of the Polio vaccine arrived clandestinely in Israel.

The Ministry of Health, together with the Polio Association members, organized a mass vaccination campaign. They later also initiated the transfer to Israel of the new vaccine developed by Professor Sabin. Before long, all the volunteers helping the young Polio victims united in one body. The new organization was called ILAN – Israel Foundation for Handicapped Children. At that time, ILAN was one of the three largest volunteer organizations in Israel.

The over fourteen thousand young Polio victims in Israel presented a challenge of the highest priority to the country's leadership. If these children were not returned to society as independent human beings, the burden on the nation would be tremendous. ILAN began to raise funds from the public. Dubiner initiated a March of Dimes, similar to the one that had taken place in the United States. Thousands of women volunteers paraded along the main streets of Israel's major cities. Instead of flags, they carried outspread blankets, into which the bystanders threw their coins and spare change.

The return to school of the child survivors presented

yet another difficult problem. The young Polio victims hobbled around on crutches or were confined to wheelchairs. The healthy children were often frightened by the sight of their disabled classmates – especially during the breaks, when the children played outside.

However, the distress of such a large population of children, seriously disabled by Polio, received scant attention. The press barely covered it. Polio was no longer newsworthy.

A STEP FORWARD

The Polio survivors' initial needs were not sport-oriented. The children encountered new obstacles; the schools and kindergartens could not provide them with physical education or recreational activities. This was a clear violation of the state's obligation to provide sports activities for all children in the framework of the general educational system. In the summer of 1953, this state of affairs motivated Betty Dubiner and her colleagues to organize summer camps in Ramat Gan and Petah Tikva. At these camps the disabled children could at least spend time together during the long school holiday, while their non-disabled friends went to the beach and on trips.

Public parks were allocated for the summer camps, equipped with wheelchairs, crutches, walkers, games, musical instruments and used tyres. Hundreds of volunteers were recruited to help take care of the disabled children. Professional sports coaches were also called in to lend a hand. Despite the spartan conditions, dozens of improvised games were adapted for the disabled children. The success of these first camps paved the way for others that followed. These were happy and exciting days for the disabled children, who suddenly found friends they could play with.

One of the participants was Baruch Hagai, a thin boy with a mop of curly hair and graceful movements. Baruch wanted friends to play with. His parents, who had immigrated to Israel from Libya not long before, with barely the clothes on their backs, had hoped he would be a footballer. That dream, of course, had been dashed by the Polio. Quick-witted and articulate Israel Globus, from Jerusalem, was paralysed from the waist down and wheelchair-bound. His religious parents had expected him to become a rabbi one day – but he yearned to play basketball. He later became a brilliant lawyer. Abraham Tshuva, who had recently left the transit camp where his family had been living since their arrival in Israel, was paralysed in both legs. This slender, shy young boy later became an important sports journalist. These disabled youngsters all yearned for companionship; they wanted to play games and practical jokes, and have fun. The summer camps helped them to realize some of their wishes. Here they were not patients under doctors' supervision or the anxious eyes of their mothers. However, the end of the long summer holiday also brought their days of happiness and fun to an end. It was time to go back to school. Confined to a wheelchair in the classroom or the street, the disabled child was an object of curiosity, fear and compassion – often being completely, and even intentionally, ignored. Like a vanquished army scattered to the winds, the disabled children returned to their homes. Their sadness at leaving the summer camp was as great as had been their joy in taking part. Autumn and winter promised nothing but cold, grey, cloudy skies and a growing feeling of distance from the world around them.

At that time, Dr. Ralph Spira, a young doctor who had recently immigrated to Israel from Great Britain, was caring for hundreds of disabled children at the Assaf Harofeh Hospital near Tel Aviv. The sheer numbers of the disabled children amazed even Spira, who was no stranger to the sight of war disabled at the Stoke Mandeville Hospital. These children needed a cheerful environment, with drawings, toys, colour and music. Many Israeli and Jewish performers from abroad volunteered to appear before this young audience – including the film star Danny Kaye, the singer and entertainer Eddie Cantor, and the king of the harmonica, Larry Adler.

The recreation rooms were decorated in particularly vibrant colours to raise the children's spirits. When the absence of a piano became painfully obvious, the ILAN

volunteers were asked to raise funds to obtain one. Betty
Dubiner appealed to her friends in New York, the
famous playwrights Sam and Bella Spewack. Before a
reply was received, good Jewish people in Israel
donated a brand new piano for the hospital. Encouraged
by this positive development, physiotherapist and coach
Gershon Huberman, a Jewish refugee from Austria,
suggested that, instead of a piano, Dubiner should ask
the Spewacks for a donation towards the establishment
of the first sports gymnasium for the disabled in Israel.
After consulting with her close friends, the artists Lois
and Arthur Elias, Bella Spewack responded favourably
to the innovative idea, and, through P.E.F. Israel
Endowment Funds in New York, sent her donation for
the construction of the first gymnasium for Israel's
disabled children.

Sam and Bella Spewack both came from poor and
traditionally Jewish families that had fled to the United
States from anti-Semitic Russia at the beginning of the
twentieth century. They were also respected journalists
with a high social awareness. During the war, Bella
had volunteered to raise funds for the children's
hospitals in the United States, and concentrated her later
efforts on the refugee children who remained stranded
in post-war Europe. As a result of their social
involvement, the Spewacks became acquainted with
President Franklin Roosevelt and his wife Eleanor.
Later, they also met President Harry Truman, who
nominated Bella as American representative to the U.N.
Rehabilitation Agency for Refugee Children. Bella went

to Poland and the Soviet Union to meet these young D.P.s. Her visits to the former Nazi extermination camps strengthened her identification with Israel. Bella Spewack also invested a considerable amount of money in The Bank of New York, intending that the interest from this investment should serve as an annual endowment to support the Centre's future everyday needs. She also nominated her close friends, actress Lois Elias, and her husband, the gifted painter Arthur Elias, as trustees of this investment. In 2009, Lois and Arthur Elias retired from this honorary position, and passed the mantle on to their daughter Minna, and son-in-law Dr. Amotz Bar-Noy.

In Israel, all that now remained was to find a suitable plot of land on which the centre could be built. Most of the Centre's founders lived in Ramat Gan. They considered their hometown to be the right location for such a facility. To this end, they approached Mayor Abraham Krinitzi with the request to allocate land. Krinitzi, who knew every inch of Ramat Gan, took the delegation to the location where the nation's first sports centre for the disabled would be built. It was a desolate piece of land on the banks of the Yarkon River, bounded by lofty eucalyptus trees. The ground was full of pits and covered with wild shrubs. The desolation of this four-acre area made it seem like forty acres. For a while, the enthusiastic promoters of the idea wondered if Krinitzi simply wanted to distance the disabled from the town and isolate the centre, but Krinitzi's logical words of persuasion won the day.

NEW HOPE FOR
THE DISABLED

The first project planned by the Centre's founders was an open-air basketball court alongside a small basketball gymnasium, to bear the names of Bella and Sam Spewack, which would serve all the disabled, without any discrimination against race, religion or gender. The gymnasium would be the first building to be constructed in the desolate location on the banks of the Yarkon River. The river flooded every winter, creating a muddy swamp. In the summer, the area was densely covered with prickly bushes. Swarms of mosquitoes filled the air. However, the urgent need of the moment was to get the construction work done quickly, simply and – above all – cheaply.

For the next eighteen months, the Centre's founders came to the site almost daily to see how work was progressing. They held their meetings on site, perched on the building blocks. Huberman was appointed professional director of the Centre. He sometimes brought a few of the disabled children with him, so that they could see what was being built for them. He would go from the construction workers to the contractor, noisily demanding improvements and changes. He almost always got his own way with his incessant requests. Even if the founders refused him, the contractor would eventually accede to his wishes – at no extra cost. As a result of the budgetary restrictions, the unplastered structure looked more like a large garage than a gymnasium. In the eyes of the exuberant promoters, however, it was a magnificent palace.

The inauguration ceremony for the Sam & Bella Spewack Gymnasium – the first facility of its kind in Israel – was held on Monday, 19 September 1960. The donors, Bella and Sam Spewack, came especially from New York City for the ceremony. They were both very proud and moved by the fact that the first gymnasium in Israel for disabled children would bear their name. As a special inauguration present, they promised Betty Dubiner that their support for the Centre would continue forever through their bequests. The committee members and other volunteers were present at the ceremony, as well as some twenty-five disabled children. Those involved felt that a supremely important historical event was taking place. Objective eyes viewed it differently.

Yedioth Ahronoth journalist, Eliyahu Amikam, reported the following day: "Mrs Bella Spewack cut the ribbon. A small audience, mostly of disabled children who had come to the celebrations from all over Israel, sat in the hall. Government ministers, mayors and public figures were conspicuous by their absence. This event had no appeal for them, it seems. Their absence did not detract from the satisfaction felt by the main celebrants, however. Mrs Dubiner was as happy as a mother hen surrounded by her chicks".

No one believed that this humble structure had anything to offer the Israeli sports community. The grey building, with its cheap, corrugated asbestos roof, and the timid children aroused only compassion. The claim that this had anything to do with sports seemed absurd in the eyes of most who, out of a desire not to offend anybody, didn't say so outright.

In an attempt to recruit participants, thousands of letters were sent to the parents of disabled children, inviting them to come. But only a few did. One who was persuaded was ten-year-old Baruch Hagai, who had already taken part in the one of the summer camps. On arriving, Hagai saw a small group of boys sitting in their wheelchairs. They were passing a ball around, but couldn't get it high enough to go into the basket. This was something that Baruch knew how to do, without any coaching.

Before coming to the Centre, Hagai had experienced humiliation at the hands of other children when he tried to take part in sports activities. On one occasion, someone had even shouted at him: "Look at him, look at the cripple...". The jibe had hurt him – but hadn't lessened his desire to keep on trying. When his classmates organized parties, he wasn't invited. "What would you do if you came?" one of the girls in his class asked him once, "You can't dance – you're a cripple". These words had made him very bitter. His hurt feelings sometimes exploded in outbursts of anger and exchanges of blows. This was the main reason why Baruch had intensified his efforts in the field of sports, finding in them a way to relieve his frustrations. Hagai's scraps with the kids at school dismayed his mother. She believed that if he would only stop trying so stubbornly to take part in sports activities, his problems would decrease. She also thought that he should be concentrating now on his studies, so that he could one day be an engineer or a lawyer. When Hagai began to spend even more time at the sports centre, his mother quarrelled with him, claiming that he was spending less time studying and more and more time on what, in her eyes, was a waste of time.

Another child who came to the Centre at that time was Itzhak Perlman. He was an attractive, smiling youngster, full of the joy of life. He also had outstanding musical talent. Both of his legs had been badly affected by Polio. His parents lived in a tiny flat in Tel Aviv, and operated a small laundry. They hoped that Itzhak would be a violinist one day, and invested any small change they could spare in violin lessons for their son. Little Itzhak, however, also wanted to be a sportsman. Many years later, Perlman did indeed become an internationally renowned violinist, and returned to visit the Centre with his father Chaim.

Coach Streifler assigned the new recruits to the groups already training on the court. He never stopped encouraging his apprehensive trainees, for whom the whole idea still seemed a little unreal. "I'll make real athletes of you yet!!" Streifler would yell at them – but only Baruch Hagai and Danny Shachar, a lively mischief-maker, were inclined to believe him. The two boys enthusiastically raced around the court on their wheelchairs, imagining that they were riding magnificent racehorses. They loved and admired their coach, Shaul Streifler, who had been inducted into the paratroopers in 1955, and completed his military service, as an officer, after being injured during the Suez Campaign. Streifler then attended a three-year course for physical education instructors at the Wingate Institute. A brief newspaper article about the sport centre for the disabled in Ramat Gan caught his eye. Here was a place where he could truly put his energies to use. He quickly made his way there. Huberman's first question was: "Would you agree to work as a volunteer for six months?" Streifler's immediate positive response got him the job.

Huberman and Streifler were concerned by the low number of disabled at the Centre. They recruited women volunteers to accompany them on home visits to families with disabled children. They also organized bonfires for disabled youngsters, roping in the parents of children who had already joined, to help and fund these events. While the young guests were eating and drinking by the bonfire, the youngsters who had already joined the Centre's activities were asked to talk about their experiences. Afterwards, the young guests were invited to look around the recently built gym, and to see disabled sports in action. These friendly methods of persuasion eventually brought results. After about a year, some fifty disabled children were regularly attending activities.

The increasing numbers of members coming to the Centre also meant growing expenses. It quickly became obvious that disabled sports required a much greater outlay than regular sports. The disabled children needed special and costly sports wheelchairs to participate. The Centre's volunteers invested much time and effort in recruiting donors for this purpose. Their endeavours were crowned with partial success, and the small number of wheelchairs obtained gave the children the mobility that they had lost. The children would come immediately after school, and train until it got dark. To diversify their activities, each athlete would train in several different sports, which naturally led to competition. In this manner, these young disabled found a way to compensate for the misfortune that fate had dealt them. Through the sports activities, they were able to express their youthful desires for speed, agility and strength. The bitterness they felt when healthy children spurned their efforts to join them in sports activities began to fade.

From a financial point of view, the Centre was an international pioneer. Israel's government had little money to spare. Even Prof. Guttman had begun his activities at Stoke Mandeville with a government budget. A similar situation prevailed in all the European countries. Yet Israel's young Polio victims received no such support. Nevertheless, the Centre continued to develop. When there was no money to pay the coaches, they worked without pay. From the experience of Coach Reuven Heller, a Wingate graduate who himself was disabled, we can learn how the coaches were recruited. In 1961, just before his demobilization as an army medic, Heller was asked to help with sports activities for the paraplegic war veterans at the Tel Hashomer Hospital. Huberman or Streifler would sometimes come and visit him, and invite him to come and see the activities at the Centre. Huberman then started persuading him to come and work with them. After he was released from the army, Heller indeed turned up, ready to start work. "Now", said Huberman, "You have to work for six months as a volunteer". Heller looked in surprise at Streifler, who nodded in acquiescence – this was indeed the custom. Heller agreed. Another recruit was Coach Otto Pfeferbaum, one of the world's best known Jewish table tennis players. He had represented the famous Jewish Hakoach club in Vienna at several Maccabiah Games.

Two years after its founding, it became clear to everyone involved that the Centre was on the verge of financial collapse. Government support was almost nonexistent. The ILAN organization was not able to provide funds for the sports activities. Expectations of additional support from the small number of overseas donors also fell short. Moreover, the immediate expenses – and the numbers of participants – were higher than had been anticipated. Honorary treasurer Baruch Breude demanded that the sports activities be curtailed – or even ended.

This of course didn't happen, and the Centre continued to exist. Some twenty years later, Baruch's son, Alon, a CPA, became chairman of ILAN – Israel Foundation for Handicapped Children, and a member of the Centre's Board of Directors.

The membership fees paid by the disabled children were a mere token, based on the social credo that no poor child should be deprived for lack of funds. The solution was to find an alternative source of funding – which could most naturally be sought in the warm hearts of Diaspora Jewry, with its strong 2000-year tradition of mutual help and social responsibility. At this juncture, the author of this book, after completing eight years as chairman of the Israel War Veterans' Organization and having gained experience of fund-raising abroad, was invited to serve as executive director of the Centre.

AGAINST THE FLOW

The Centre's training programme now revolved mainly around the large, newly constructed open-air swimming pool (which would be renovated twenty-five years later through a donation from the Milken Family Foundation). Training sessions were held also for track and field events, table tennis and basketball. In 1962, Coach Streifler announced that he would be choosing a team of six athletes, based on merit, to take part in the Stoke Mandeville Games. Whoever wanted to be part of the team would have to make an extra effort.

At Stoke Mandeville, the six young basketball players he chose were accommodated in a large dormitory. Forty beds were crammed into each of several such dormitories – almost like in wartime. However, the gloomy atmosphere of the war years was replaced by one of joy at the thought of the coming games, in which 255 participants from twenty countries were taking part. The Israeli group was the youngest, most of the athletes being in their mid-teens. The average age of the other delegations, mostly World War II disabled, was around 32. For this reason, the young Israeli athletes received a condescending welcome from their older counterparts. "What are you kids doing here?" one of the athletes from the hosting British team tossed at them. This veteran sportsman would quickly discover the calibre of these youngsters.

Within a few days, the derisive comments turned into amazement. The Israeli team was the surprise of the 1962 games. The novices from Israel beat the British team, considered at that time to be one of the best in the world, and other strong international teams. On its way to the semi-finals, Israel beat the Belgian team with a score of over 100 – the highest international score ever achieved at that time in wheelchair basketball. The conditions then were very different from today: the wheelchairs were heavy, and the game lasted for forty minutes – with no time outs. The Israeli team met the strong Italian team in the semi-finals. The score was even at the end of time, and remained so even after a double overtime. Two Israeli players had been sent off and there were now no substitute players on the bench to replace them. The Italians eventually beat Israel by one point.

Baruch Hagai's outstanding talents came to the fore in these international basketball games. He proved to be an agile player with great leadership skills, both in the concept of the game itself and also in his amazing accuracy in shooting the ball. Hagai was also blessed with a fighting spirit and courage that never failed him, even at moments when it seemed that all was lost. Players from all over the world sought to emulate his special style of playing. This unknown boy from Israel very quickly became a familiar figure in the world of wheelchair basketball. Hagai also drew on his wheelchair skills to play table tennis, developing a swift volley and his own unique style. He gave even experienced players stiff competition. When he returned to Israel, tired and worn out from the Stoke Mandeville Games, his mother soon saw that her son had changed. His bitterness had faded. The day after he returned, still exhausted, but enjoying a day off with his mother's culinary attentions, she suddenly asked him: "What's the matter with you, Baruch? Aren't you going to the Centre today?" Despite his fatigue, he was very happy to hear his mother's words. With the last of his energy, he left the house for another long day of training – which he knew would replenish his reserves.

The first wheelchair basketball league in Israel was now established at the Centre. Since less than thirty athletes played wheelchair basketball, a special league of only three-member teams was organized. Seven teams participated in the league, and competed against each other every week.

That same year, with the help of his kibbutz friends, Coach Streifler organized a summer camp at Kibbutz Nir Eliyahu. He announced that every athlete who wanted to take part in the 1963 Stoke Mandeville Games had to participate in this training camp, which was also intended to strengthen the group's spirit and social unity. The kids had to do their share of hard work in the mornings. A dozen young disabled athletes took part in this camp. Their days started at five in the morning, when Streifler would wake them. After the boys had finished washing and tidying their beds, they devoted an hour to physical exercises in their wheelchairs. After a seven o'clock breakfast, the young athletes would then do their work tasks around the kibbutz until one o'clock. Immediately after lunch, they would begin their training sessions, which went on continuously until seven in the evening. After showers and an evening meal, they would sit down to listen to discussions on tactics. The kids would sometimes doze off out of sheer exhaustion. No medicine or treatment could have better motivated these young paraplegics, to get so much out of their injured bodies, than sports.

Streifler was getting ready to leave the Centre in 1963. He planned to study economics at university in Chicago, and wanted the basketball team to be in peak condition before he left. To this end, he organized an additional training camp in England, a week before the Stoke Mandeville Games. The site they found was a training school for dog handlers, known as "The Dog House". Streifler repeatedly made his team go over the gruelling exercises to increase their stamina. The Israeli athletes, who had to train and sweat all day (from six in the morning until seven in the evening), and who ached all over, were often jealous of the pampered dogs, which lazed around comfortably in their kennels.

In their first five games, the Centre's team beat England, Sweden, France, Switzerland and Belgium. The team was due to meet Italy in the semi-finals. The Italians asked for the game to be deferred three times for technical reasons. When the Israeli lads finally got to the court, they were surprised to discover that they had no team to play against. The referees announced a technical win. In the finals, the Israelis met the world champion American team. About seven hundred spectators crowded around the open-air basketball court – a record audience for a wheelchair basketball game at Stoke Mandeville. The game was balanced and swift. Baruch Hagai was once again at his best. The Americans eventually succeeded in winning the championship by one point.

The table tennis games took place in a large marquee. It was so hot inside the big tent that it was almost like being in a greenhouse. Despite the heat, Baruch Hagai won his first world championship for table tennis.

Towards the end of 1963, the Centre's basketball team gained additional international experience. In cooperation with the resident manager of Pan American Airlines, Wesley Aarons whose daughter, Sharona, later married Arthur Broza, Betty Dubiner and Arthur Broza arranged for the Pan American Jets – one of the strongest

American wheelchair basketball teams – to visit Israel, and play friendly games.

The development of sports activities at the Centre aroused a great deal of interest abroad, and especially in the United States. In 1965, the U.S. Ministry of Health funded research on the influence of sports activities on disabled children in Israel. Dr. Ralph Spira carried out this research at the Centre between 1965-66. Doctors and social psychologists observed two groups over a two-year period. Each group comprised about fifty children aged between seven and ten, who suffered from similar disabilities as a result of Polio. Only one of the groups participated in sports activities. The results of the tests showed a clear difference between the physical and psychological condition of the children in each of the two groups. The group taking part in sports activities displayed greater self-confidence and self-discipline and, most importantly, they did better at their studies and were more socially active. Physically, the children who took part in sports activities showed a far more developed musculature, especially of the upper body.

The President, Prof. Ephraim Katzir, who was briefed on these developments, expressed his desire to come and meet the disabled athletes. He was very impressed by his visit, and coined the famous phrase: "I came to encourage – instead, I was encouraged".

The numbers of disabled children joining the Centre increased, and the categories of disability became more varied. There were now twelve separate fields of wheelchair sport being operated at the Centre.

A MIRACLE IN RAMAT GAN

After an interim of more than two millennia, the
Olympic Games were revived, in 1896, on the initiative
of the French baron, Pierre de Coubertin. De Coubertin
wanted to bring the ancient Greeks' Olympic ideals to
life, and to develop them into a movement that
transcended national boundaries. The media showcased
de Coubertin's achievements to a degree beyond all
expectations. In a few short years, ever thirsty for new
idols, the media glorified the image of the new sports
heroes, turning them into legendary icons. Professor
Guttman understood that if his innovative disabled
sports movement could be integrated into this general
sports trend, it would also benefit. To this end, he

applied to the International Olympic Committee (IOC) at the end of the 1950s, with the request that disabled sports be recognized as an integral part of the international Olympic movement.

The IOC gave an ostensibly positive response, agreeing to hold international games for the disabled immediately following the traditional Olympic Games, but without giving the event any official recognition. However, during the 1956 Melbourne Olympics, the IOC presented the Fearnley Cup (which was awarded to governments and bodies that had contributed to the promotion of the Olympic spirit) to the Stoke Mandeville Games. Guttman understood this act to mean that the way was now paved for the "Olympic Games for the Disabled" or the "Paralympics", as it became known, to be held immediately after the 1960 Rome Olympics. And, indeed, four hundred disabled athletes from twenty-three nations took part in these Games. The second Paralympics took place four years later in Tokyo, with three hundred and ninety participants from twenty-two countries.

In 1968, the third Paralympics should have been held in Mexico. About a year before the Games, the Mexican organizing committee announced that, as a result of financial difficulties, it would be unable to host the event. Following this development, Guttman sent appeals to various countries, including Israel, asking them to host the Paralympics. The only country to rise to the challenge was Israel – mainly because of Huberman's enthusiasm, backed by ILAN

representatives. However, the body that officially
undertook responsibility for organizing the Games was
the Israel Sports Association for the Disabled, most of
whose representatives were members of the Centre. The
Association was chaired by Arieh Fink, who headed
the rehabilitation division of the Ministry of Defence.
Many countries announced their participation.
However, no practical plan had been formulated for the
absorption of the large number of disabled athletes who
registered. In the meantime, the Six-Day War of 1967
broke out. In view of the financial distress in which
Israel now found itself, it seemed that it would be
impossible to obtain even the small amount of funding
that had been hoped for. Yosef Ovad was elected to
take over as executive director of the Israeli committee.
Ovad was one of the promoters of disabled sport for
disabled war veterans. As a seaman, he was accustomed
to solving problems and worked well under pressure.
His fine qualities were eminently suited to the job at
hand. Ovad at once began working energetically to
recruit hundreds of volunteers, specialists and
professionals, for the various committees.

As there were only a small number of wheelchair-
accessible rooms in the hotels of the Greater Tel Aviv
area, suitable accommodation had to be prepared. In
order to overcome this obstacle, Ovad sought hotels
that would agree to convert large numbers of rooms,
making them suitable for the disabled athletes. Ovad
also set about solving the transportation problem. He
asked the paraplegic ex-serviceman Zvi Ben-Zvi to help

him examine different bus models, but found none with a raising and lowering mechanism. Ovad finally solved the problem when he saw a bus with a wide central entrance. He quickly sketched a ramp that could be attached to the bus doorway, so that wheelchairs could be rolled on and off the bus.

The Israeli army responded favourably to the idea of involving soldiers in taking care of the foreign guests in the actual operation of the Paralympics. This involvement emphasized the human side of the Israel Defence Forces (IDF), and its willingness to help with social assignments. The race against time continued as growing numbers of foreign athletes registered for the Paralympics. About two weeks before the opening, over eight hundred athletes had confirmed their participation, and the number of nations attending had reached twenty-nine. It became clear that this was to be the largest Paralympics so far, and Ovad found himself forced to go over the allocated budget.

Israel's delegation comprised sixty athletes. The Israeli athletes naturally wanted to stay at the Kfar Hamaccabiah Hotel, together with the other athletes – but there were not enough rooms available. The Paralympics Committee felt that the atmosphere would be spoiled if the competing athletes were not all accommodated together, enabling the Israeli athletes to socialize with their foreign counterparts. The large Israeli delegation was therefore eventually packed into the hotel storerooms, which were filled with folding camp beds – each used by two or three of the Israeli athletes in rotation.

The opening ceremony of the Paralympics was held on Monday, 4 November 1968 in the stadium of the Hebrew University of Jerusalem, in front of twenty-four thousand spectators. Deputy Prime Minister Yigal Allon attended the ceremony in lieu of President Shazar, who had fallen ill. Allon took his place on the podium together with Mayor of Jerusalem Teddy Kollek and other Israeli VIPs. The delegations then entered the stadium, headed by Charles Atkinson of Great Britain and Gershon Huberman of Israel, followed by the wheelchair-confined disabled athletes of all nationalities in their colourful uniforms.

Young Israeli scouts lit hundreds of blazing torches in the stadium after the delegations had lined themselves up on the huge turf. Three dance troupes, three choirs and an army orchestra provided a brief musical overture to the opening ceremony. The scouts raised three flags: the flag of the State of Israel, the Olympic flag, and the flag of the Stoke Mandeville Games. Just as Deputy Prime Minister Allon completed his speech, hundreds of white doves were released into the air. The captain of the Israeli delegation, disabled war veteran Zvi Ben-Zvi swore the Olympic oath.

For most of the Christian guests, the Holy Land evoked deeply religious feelings linked to the salvation of disabled and suffering individuals. The holy city of Jerusalem and neighbouring Bethlehem, the birthplace of Jesus, had a particularly emotional significance. Biblical events seemed very close at hand. The Christian participants were reminded of the suffering and affliction of Jesus and his disciples. The sight of the disabled athletes, appearing, row after row, seemed to present an image of tortured beings, nailed to their wheelchairs. It even appeared to some as if Jesus' miracles were being performed again, this time by a modern saviour – Jewish, like Jesus – offering redemption to today's disabled victims. This disciple had also been persecuted by an evil and mighty regime – the murderous Third Reich. Many felt as though they were taking part in a euphoric scene, instilled with the hope of resurrection: rehabilitation, justice and triumph of the spirit.

The twenty-four thousand Israeli spectators, the largest Paralympic audience so far, saw the event differently. While the Jewish people believed that Israel had been miraculously saved during the Six-Day War, Israel's citizens were very much aware of the immense human cost. The Israeli public identified with the disabled sports movement and its pioneering achievements in rehabilitating the disabled. Many, in fact, believed that Israel was fulfilling its role as "a beacon to the nations".

Despite the success of the opening ceremony, the ten days of competitions at the modest facilities of the Centre and the adjoining National Stadium were austerity itself. The Israeli athletes had to bring their clothing from home. Baruch Hagai was a basketball player, and his shirt bore the number 11. This shirt had already become an object of anxiety to wheelchair basketball teams all over the world. After playing basketball, Hagai hurried off to play table tennis, wearing the same shirt. There, too, his rivals learned to recognize the No. 11 shirt. Baruch would wash his shirt in the evening, after the competitions, wringing it out in his hands and drying it in the warm Israeli air. Ironing was done army fashion – by leaving the straightened-out shirt under the mattress all night. The tale of the No. 11 shirt reflects the conditions under which the Israeli delegation operated.

Hagai wore this same shirt for the wheelchair basketball final, which took place on the Centre's open-air basketball court. Amazingly, about six thousand spectators managed to find a perch on the temporary seating that had been erected. The festive atmosphere and large crowd fired the Israeli team with enthusiasm. Under Coach Reuven Heller, they played a swift, efficient and enduring game. It was their best game ever. Israel's gallant team won 47:37 against the American favourites. The guests of honour at this event, charismatic Minister of Defence Moshe Dayan, and the American Ambassador, Walworth Barbour, awarded medals to the two teams. The Cup was presented to athlete Danny Shachar, captain of the Israeli team. The Israeli women's wheelchair basketball team, too, under Coach Moshe Rosenberg, took first place and won a Paralympic gold medal.

The Paralympics held in Israel were the first in which over a thousand athletes, coaches and escorts participated. Israel's athletes displayed a far greater ability than could have been expected from a country with such a small population. Israel established its standing as a major player in the international disabled sports arena, winning a total of 22 gold, 20 silver and 24 bronze medals. There was also great camaraderie between the disabled sportsmen of all the participating countries. In the past, the members of each delegation had generally kept their own company. In the warm atmosphere they found in Israel, the national team barrier faded away.

After the Paralympics, the attitude towards disabled sport in Israel became more accepting. These Games had proved to be an effective vehicle for presenting disabled sports to a wider public. Many journalists who had previously ignored the existence of disabled sports now began to report on them. But the most important advance was the one that took place in the hearts of the disabled themselves. The results of the 1968 Paralympics were proof of the high level of disabled sport in Israel, which brought great honour, recognition and pride to the State of Israel.

There was also a growing awareness of the Centre's accomplishments among Jews abroad. With the support received, it was now possible to construct many new facilities. In order to oversee these new constructions, Engineer David Weinreb, a disabled athlete and economic entrepreneur, who served on the Board of Directors, was nominated as the Centre's honorary development and construction consultant.

THE CHAMPION

Baruch Hagai is the most famous wheelchair basketball player the world has ever known. His love of basketball was evident from the very beginning, just from the way he held the ball. He had the same caring attitude towards his wheelchair, and would put aside a special time each day for its maintenance. Hagai was an athletic virtuoso, in the same way that Itzhak Perlman – who at one time trained together with him – became a musical virtuoso. As Baruch rolled onto the basketball court in his wheelchair, he was overcome by a kind of fever. No basketball player could stop him – by fair means. He was the master of evasive strategy. He inspired his team-mates, and provided a personal example of hard work and a readiness for self-sacrifice. He was always the first to arrive at training sessions – and the last to leave. He constantly urged his fellow team-mates on, to do better and move even faster, and to be united as a group determined to win. His greatness was revealed precisely at those difficult moments when it seemed that all was lost. Baruch never came to terms with defeat. He knew only how to fill his team-mates with confidence – sweeping them along after him, dispelling their feelings of despair and strengthening their spirit, to turn an apparent defeat into a victory.

During the game, Hagai's face was alight with vigour, reflecting the entire gamut of his emotions: determination, fury, regret, admiration, satisfaction, gratitude and, sometimes, even resentment against an unfair referee or a fouling rival. When the coach sent him off court, to rest or calm down, his face reflected his surprise and protest against what he was sure was the coach's mistake. He found it difficult to reconcile himself to the fact that the team was playing without him. He would try to hide his feelings by taking part in the game from the bench, firing words of encouragement at his friends.

For twenty-five years, he struck fear into the hearts of Israel's sports rivals in the international arena. The coaches of the opposing teams planned their game tactics with the objective of blocking Hagai, often neglecting the rest of the team. Hagai never resented his team-mates' success, and would jest with his personal "bodyguards", charging his way through them and passing the ball to another Israeli player who was free to shoot the ball. His strained and sweating features bore witness to the effort he put into the game and into manoeuvring his cumbersome wheelchair – which, at that time, weighed somewhere between eleven and eighteen kilograms.

Hagai had an enormous influence on the development of wheelchair basketball, both in Israel and abroad. He was a pioneer in the field of offensive tactics, and was able to manoeuvre his wheelchair with great speed and dexterity, developing many new strategies. He was the master of long shots. Most importantly, he was a natural leader and a sensitive, intelligent player, with the ability to analyse the game – while playing. Under Hagai's leadership, Israel's national wheelchair basketball team won two gold and two silver Paralympic medals. He also led the team to victory in four World Championships, one World Cup and two European Championships. He was at his best in the games against the United States, a country that promoted the best wheelchair basketball in the world.

The entire development of Israeli wheelchair basketball and its achievements in the world arena can be seen through Baruch Hagai's eyes. After he joined the team in 1962, Israel's wheelchair basketball began to make a name for itself in the disabled sports arena, performing outstandingly at the Stoke Mandeville Games. Despite the fact that the Israeli wheelchair basketball team had come to Tokyo without its full contingent, it took third place in the 1964 Paralympics held there. Baruch was the No. 1 Israeli player on the court for all of these games.

In 1964, an official basketball league was organized, consisting of six teams from the Centre and two from the Israel War Veterans' Organization. Hagai was the pivotal player of the Ramat Gan team, which presented a significant challenge to the other seven teams. The sweeping victories and the harsh confrontations provided fertile ground for new basketball players to develop. The league that had been created in 1964 developed and expanded over the years into a twenty-five team basketball league.

Following the international successes of the Centre's basketball team, Benjamin Lipton, one of the founders of wheelchair sports in the United States, invited the Centre's team in 1971, for a series of friendly games against American and Canadian wheelchair basketball teams. Seventeen American teams and three Canadian teams were included in the tight schedule. During the twenty-two days of its visit to the United States, the Israeli team played twenty games. Despite the pressure of time and the need sometimes to play twice on one day, the Israeli team displayed outstanding abilities, and racked up seventeen wins.

In 1974, the Stoke Mandeville Games was recognized as the wheelchair basketball world championship. The Israeli team, coached by Reuven Heller, was then at the very peak of its success. It won the world championship at Stoke Mandeville after beating the U.S. team 52:47. The Israelis showed their

88

Doomed to Glory

superiority again at the World Cup games in Bruges, when they won the World Cup, again against the American team – 60:47.

Baruch Hagai completed twenty-five years of wheelchair basketball in the uniform of the Israeli national team – an unprecedented sports record. Baruch also notched up additional achievements when a forum of international sports coaches selected him as the most outstanding disabled athlete in the world both for the 1970s and for the 1980s. At the 1980 Paralympics, this same forum voted Coach Reuven Heller the most outstanding coach for disabled athletes in the world. When Hagai returned the Israeli national team's No. 11 shirt after the Seoul Olympics in 1988, he had achieved yet another Israeli and world record – he had played 224 international wheelchair basketball games in the national team's uniform, and another 66 international games in the Centre's uniform. In these international games, he had scored 6,078 points and caught 2,016 rebounds. In addition, he had scored 13,512 points in 563 Israeli national basketball league games, catching 6,756 rebounds. His average score was 21 in international games and 24 in local games. His average number of assists was 8, and rebounds – 12. Altogether, he scored a total of 19,598 points, catching 10,236 rebounds, with 6,824 assists.

Hagai's outstanding wheelchair basketball legacy lives on in the dozens of young wheelchair basketball players who seek to emulate his special style, and play "just like Baruch". He continues to play in the

framework of ILAN – Ramat Gan. From 1990 until
1994, he also coached Israel's national wheelchair
basketball team.

In addition to playing basketball, Hagai also swam
and was an outstanding table tennis player. He began
table tennis training in 1961. Coach Otto Pfeferbaum
carefully selected his trainees from among the most
disciplined, conscientious and resolute athletes. Hagai
developed an innovative method of playing. Until that
time, wheelchair table tennis players had sat very close
to the table, so that the ball only had a short distance to
travel. By moving his wheelchair quickly from side to
side, he could roll swiftly backwards from the table in
his wheelchair – thus increasing the distance the ball
had to travel and, of course, adding great excitement
and interest to the game.

At his first Stoke Mandeville appearance in 1962,
Hagai lost only in the finals match against the Italian
champion, Berghella. It was clear to everyone that he
was a rising star. In 1963, he beat Berghella in the finals
at Stoke Mandeville, and took the world championship
title. Hagai's next goal was the Tokyo Paralympics in
1964, where he beat the Japanese champion and won
the gold medal. In the 1968 Paralympics, which were
held in Israel, Hagai again took the table tennis gold
medal and, together with his friend, Arye Rubin, also
won the Doubles gold medal.

It seemed as if Hagai's supremacy at the table tennis
table would last forever. But then the talented American
player, Mike Dempsey, whose star began to rise in the

1970s, became a challenge. Dempsey was short and thin, with heavily muscled arms. He usually won his matches with a score of 2:0. The battle of these two world wheelchair table tennis stars took place at the 1972 Heidelberg Paralympics. Dempsey had won all his Heidelberg matches outright – 2:0, while Hagai had won his matches only by a small margin. In the finals, Hagai had to face an opponent with glittering achievements. The match took place in a hall filled to overflowing with five thousand spectators – all of whom seemed to think that the day belonged to Dempsey. Baruch Hagai had other ideas. He began the game diffidently, with short weak shots. Everybody was used to his far-reaching jet-propelled serves. His serves here were shorter, and the ball bounced close to the net. These serves were catastrophic for Dempsey. With his lack of height and short arms, he found it almost impossible to reach the ball. The match ended at 0:2 to Hagai's advantage, and he garnered another gold medal.

As anticipated, the pair reached the finals at the 1973 Stoke Mandeville Games. This time, Dempsey had prepared a surprise of his own: a table tennis racket with a long handle. This gave him a longer reach, enabling him to return serves bouncing close to the net. In this match, however, Hagai displayed his resourcefulness and skill to the full. Instead of short shots, he returned to his method of distancing himself from the table and hitting long, powerful shots. Dempsey, with his long racket, had no choice but to move back, away from the table. The advantage he had hoped to gain turned into a disadvantage. Hagai won the day yet again.

Dempsey and Hagai met once again in 1976, at the Paralympic wheelchair table tennis finals in Toronto. This match took place on a large court, where the wheelchair basketball final between Israel and the United States was scheduled to take place immediately afterwards. The courtyard, which seated four thousand, was packed, and included Canadian government representatives and the Israeli delegation's sponsor, Murray Goldman from Toronto. Contrary to expectations, the table tennis match itself was very tense, although Baruch succeeded in beating Dempsey 2:0. A fourth consecutive Paralympic win was an extraordinary occurrence. At the end of the match, Coach Otto Pfeferburg jumped up to hug his protégé, shouting: "You're going out like a champion, Baruch – You're retiring like a champion!". Hagai emotionally confirmed Otto's declaration in front of the television cameras that surrounded him.

Although Hagai retired from international table tennis competitions, he still coaches table tennis at the Centre. When his involvement in international table tennis ceased at the end of the 1970s, Hagai's attention turned to regular tennis, which was just beginning at the Centre. With his athletic talents and his superb control over the wheelchair, he soon became an outstanding tennis player, often using his unique ability to dishearten players who were technically better than he was. Since 1982, when wheelchair tennis championships began in Israel, Hagai won the championship title ten times.

Although Hagai has retired from the international wheelchair sports arena, since 1985 he has held the position of Head Coach at the Centre, working about eight hours a day on a volunteer basis. He is also an active member of the Board of Directors. He passes on to others his perception of sport as a source of enriching and exciting personal experience, and a tool for self-improvement. His glittering sports achievements led to his being included in the Jewish Sports Hall of Fame. Hagai's voluntary work can best be seen as an expression of his feelings of great debt to the Centre, which took him in as a young, frustrated disabled boy, and helped him to mature into a self-confident man. He is now settling that debt in full. His life's experience has taught him how important sport is to thousands of disabled, and especially to the children – for whom the Centre is a pivotal factor in changing and shaping the course of their lives. The highpoint of Baruch's recognition was reached in 2001, when the President of the State of Israel awarded him the Israel Prize, the most highly regarded award of public recognition, for his outstanding contributions to the Israeli sports community – and three decades of great sportsmanship and personal example.

III

REAL SPORTS
HEROES

VICTIMS OF HUMAN EVIL

In addition to the physical and psychological injuries caused by nature, recent years have borne witness to more and more injuries caused by human evil.

Asa'el Shabbo was seriously wounded a few years ago, when he was nine years old. A barbarous Palestinian terrorist group broke into the family home on the Itamar settlement. The terrorists murdered Asa'el's mother Rachel, and three of his siblings: five-year-old Avishai, eleven-year-old Zvi, and sixteen-year-old Neria. Asa'el also lost a leg in the attack. This tragedy left traumatic scars on the little boy's soul.

Losing his leg was not Asa'el's major problem. The

pain, grief and shock of the terrible moments of losing
his mother and three siblings drove him into a constant,
terrible state of mourning. The hammering of the fatal
shots during those terrible moments when his family
was murdered resounded repeatedly inside his head.
Again and again he saw the fire that broke out in his
home, and the screaming and the agonised, dying cries
of his mother and siblings assaulted his ears.

He became a very sad and solitary child. He kept his
distance from those around him – and spoke to almost
nobody apart from his father. When people tried to make
contact with him, they sensed his hostility, as if he was
angry with them. What he really felt at that time was a
maelstrom of emotions – anger, pain and also a desire
for revenge. Apart from these emotions, the outside
world didn't exist for him.

When Asa'el was invited to join the Centre, his father,
Boaz, wasn't optimistic. He didn't think that sports
activities could help his son. However, after visiting
the Centre, and seeing Asa'el hesitantly playing
wheelchair basketball with other disabled kids, his
scepticism was countered. Boaz hoped that the contact
with other disabled children, and Asa'el's desire to play
with them, would help his son conquer his depression.
He saw his son playing again – and even grinning when
he scored a basket. His family, and especially his father,
Boaz, actively encouraged Asa'el to spend time at the
Centre. Asa'el trained several times a week, surrounded
by understanding and love. In the years since his great
loss and injury, he has persevered and become one of

the top swimmers in his age group, winning bronze, silver and – recently – a gold medal. His state of mind improved. Sport activities helped him to grow stronger, and enabled him to live with the pain and the memories. He represented the Centre on a fund-raising mission to New York, at the office of ISCD friend and supporter, Michael Steinhardt. Over the years, through his sports activities, Asa'el has gained mental strength and renewed his spirit and energies. He is now able to smile more often. He has matured into a strong and self-confident young man. As such, the ISCD asked him to visit recent disabled terror victims, and try to persuade them to join the Centre's sports activities. Asa'el was very successful in this new mission. He has visited young terror victims in hospital and at their homes. This is how he came to meet disabled terror victims from Sderot, including the two Tuito brothers, at the Tel Hashomer Hospital. He convinced them to join the Centre, and accompanied them on their first visits.

Asa'el has moved on from being a helpless terror victim to being an assistant coach at the Centre, concentrating his activities on those who share his traumatic fate – the young disabled terror victims.

***

The two Tuito brothers, Osher and Rami, were severely injured by one of the Kassam rockets fired at the southern town of Sderot by Hamas terrorists. The younger brother, Osher, lost a leg. His second leg was very severely wounded. Rami suffered serious injuries in both legs. The two brothers sank into a deep depression, and were terrified of what the future had in store for them. Asa'el Shabbo, who visited them in hospital, knew from his own painful personal experience that what was now needed to advance the two brothers' rehabilitation was a stimulating change in their tedious routine. He was sure that joining the Centre would revive and replenish their spirits.

The unique point in this episode is the fact that the person who motivated the disabled brothers to take this important step in their rehabilitation process was none other than Asa'el Shabbo – the same small disabled boy who, seven years earlier, was just like them – helpless and broken-spirited. Now he is able to uplift the spirits of newly disabled youngsters who share his fate, and help them on their long and demanding journey to rehabilitation.

***

Elad Wassa was seriously wounded when a terrorist explosive device was detonated in the Netanya city market. He suffered very severe burns and also injuries to his spine, resulting in the paralysis of his lower body.

Elad was born in Ethiopia. After walking with his eight-member family about a thousand kilometres to a refugee camp in the Sudan, he was brought to Israel in 1984 in the framework of "Operation Moses" – during which over eight thousand Ethiopian Jews were airlifted to Israel. Nate Shapiro, Vice President of the ISCD's Midwest Friends' Committee and President of the American Association for the Jews of Ethiopia, was one of the people behind this operation. During Elad's school years, he successfully took part in long-distance races. However, deep in his heart, once in Israel, he dreamt of emulating Michael Jordan, whose photograph he kept under his pillow in the childish hope that some of Jordan's qualities would be transferred to him. However, the maturing Elad needed to find employment to help support his family, and he began working as a porter in the Netanya market.

His career as a market worker was brought to an abrupt end by the terrorist explosive. Once his injuries had sufficiently healed, he insisted on sitting in a wheelchair and moving around. His optimistic and energetic personality won him many friends and, after completing his medical treatments at the hospital, he quickly found his way to the Centre. Baruch Hagai, the ISCD's Head Coach and Israel Prize recipient said: "There is in Elad a great talent for sports and a very strong spirit. In spite of his severe injuries, his rehabilitation will be relatively quick".

As a religious young Jew and a disabled victim of Palestinian terror, Wassa's life story made him the right person to meet with Christopher Reeve, during the latter's visit to Israel. "Superman" was anxious to talk with victims of Palestinian terror. He heard Wassa's story, and praised him for his sporting spirit.

"I'm also a sportsman", said Reeve, "and, as a

sportsman, I always try to do the very best I can, without giving up". Reeve was badly injured in a sports accident, when he was thrown off a galloping horse. He unfortunately died a year after his visit to Israel.

***

Fifteen-year-old Eli Samira was a tall, good-looking and popular boy. He was a successful athlete and a good student, seemingly with his whole life in front of him. He was planning on joining the Israeli air force, and becoming a pilot.

All Eli wanted to do that sunny afternoon was to meet his classmates at the Carmel Market in Tel Aviv, quite a distance from his home. He got on the bus – but never made the meeting…. Instead, a mighty flash of light overwhelmed him, and plunged him into a deep pit of darkness. The media dispassionately reported that a Palestinian terrorist had blown up a bus in Tel Aviv. Fourteen people had been killed and over forty injured. Eli Samira's name appeared amongst the names of the severely injured.

The doctors at Ichilov Hospital didn't give Eli's shocked parents any hope at all. He had devastating injuries to his head and throat, and was in a very deep coma. One of the living dead, with a machine breathing for him, and tubes going in and out of his body to keep him alive. No hope. The "best case scenario" was that Eli could continue to live "like a vegetable" for the rest of his life. In fact, for the next three years he was indeed a "vegetable"; his face and body were ashen, like dried leaves. His parents were constantly at his bedside, caressing him, hugging him, speaking to him. They refused to believe that he couldn't feel or hear anything. They believed in miracles, and were convinced that their love and devotion would bring Eli back to life again.

And a miracle indeed happened. Three years after his devastating injury, Eli slowly opened his eyes and tried to clear his throat. As if through a dense fog, he saw the blurred faces of his parents and the dazzling white walls. He tried to move, but his arms and legs wouldn't obey him. The clogging saliva that had gathered in his throat almost choked him. His unexpected awakening was a miracle that brought all the doctors and nurses to his bedside.

Eli couldn't understand what had happened. All he could hear and feel was a sharp hammering in his head. At that moment, the only thing he wanted to do was to escape the terrible pain. In time, he was gradually disconnected from the tubes and machines. Every tiny step forward demanded immense and excruciatingly painful efforts that exhausted and drained him.

After many months of therapy, Eli was able to express himself by making sounds, but he still couldn't say what he really wanted. He wanted to ask exactly what had happened. His parents tried to explain, and optimistically told him that everything would eventually be fine. Eli, however, felt powerless to cope with the multitude of difficulties facing him. For even the simplest actions, like eating, he was dependent on someone else's help. The only thing he wanted to do was to sleep. However, he agreed to do as his parents urged, and continued with the endless treatments.

Eli's progress was very slow, but he did begin to regain some of the abilities he had lost. He was taught to speak again, but his voice was weak and his speech halting. Some of his old friends from school came to visit him, and tried to refresh his memories. But the girl he had loved, and who he thought had loved him, disappeared – leaving him with scarred emotions. He was very aware of the wonderful life that should have been, and that had passed him by. Eli is no longer the person he was. His disappointment has weakened his stronger emotions, like anger, ambition and desire. He is resigned to his fate – his personality completely changed by the explosive blast.

Eli's parents brought him to the Centre to start rehabilitative sport therapy. The coaches have gradually observed a slight improvement in his condition. But does Eli really want to take part in the sports activities? Bringing him to the Centre was his parents' idea, in the same way that they work with him and urge him to regain some of the faculties he has lost. They are substituting – they hope temporarily – for Eli's own will to overcome the physical and psychological obstacles he now has to confront. His parents believe that sports activities, in addition to the medical treatment he is receiving at the renowned Re'ut Neurological Medical Centre, the Rehab Unit of which is headed by

Professor Avi Ori, will give him something to live for. They know there is still a very long way to go.

***

Sports activities contribute to the confidence and self-image of the disabled more than any other form of rehabilitation. The Centre serves as an international pioneer for professionals all over the world – including the United States, the United Kingdom, Germany, Sweden, Holland and Russia – who view the ISCD as a model, and send their coaches and disabled athletes to study the Centre's methods

Ryan Martin, from Washington, D.C., was only twelve when he became a paraplegic, completely confined to a wheelchair. How did it happen? As Sari Horwitz graphically wrote, in *The Washington Post* of 1 October 1999: "Martin once thought he could be a professional soccer player, and he might have made it. At 12, he was a star on the field, driven by his love of competition and the game. But on Jan. 21, 1987, the boy and his parents and little brother pulled up to their Northwest Washington home, and a man with a gun was waiting. The estranged boyfriend of the family's former nanny had stalked the family for weeks; she had disappeared, and he blamed them. The man stepped out of his car, aimed the gun at Ryan's stepfather, fired three times and missed. Then he turned toward Ryan. Ryan didn't hear the gunshots or feel the bullets ripping into his

back. But even though it was a cold night and about to
snow, lying on the ground he felt an intense wave of
heat move through his body. Fekadu Abtew had shot
Ryan twice and then driven off. Abtew ended up in a
Baltimore bar, where he shot and killed himself. The
story was all over the news. Ryan Martin almost died
that night. Finally, a doctor at Children's Hospital told
his parents: Your son will make it, but he will live the
rest of his life paralyzed from the waist down."

Unable to walk but undaunted in spirit, Martin, who
had been an excellent athlete before the shooting, was
determined to return to activity. He continued his Bar
Mitzvah studies by telephone in his hospital room, and
later took up wheelchair tennis. His valiant attitude
caught the attention of Alan Sherman, then vice
president of the U.S. Committee/ Sports for Israel.
Sherman felt that Martin could benefit from the Centre's
work, and, in 1988, sponsored a trip to Israel for him
and his mother, Sharan. Martin's wheelchair tennis
game quickly improved with the coaching of the
Centre's Baruch Hagai, then a top wheelchair tennis
player – ranked third in the world. Martin's enthusiasm
and commitment during the training sessions were
tremendous. Before long, the boy was helping out at
the Centre as an assistant coach, working with the
younger disabled children, and also playing wheelchair
table tennis and basketball.

When the time came for Martin to return to his
Washington home, the Centre's disabled children parted

from him and his mother with great warmth. There were many hugs and kisses – especially from the girls. Surrounded by friends and admirers, Martin listened to the words of Coach Baruch Hagai: "You are a great athlete, Ryan. You have tremendous spirit. With hard work and your natural athletic talent, I'm sure that we will be hearing lots more about you in the future". This indeed was the case.

After he returned to the family home in Washington, Martin organized a committee of disabled American youngsters to support the Centre. Each one donated a few cents to the amazing sports centre that their friend described so vividly. This reflected Martin's personality and his feelings of gratitude to those who had helped him. He continued training in American wheelchair sports clubs, mainly tennis and basketball. He soon became recognized as an outstanding athlete in both these sports. He won many gold medals in U.S. national wheelchair tennis competitions – winning the U.S. Open at the tender age of fifteen. He also played on several excellent U.S. wheelchair basketball teams, including N.W. West All-Star Team.

Ryan understood that his future life would depend on his acquiring a profession that would enable him to support himself and his future family, and make a meaningful and rewarding contribution to society. He felt that sport was an auxiliary device, which would help him to cope with his future responsibilities. He chose medicine as the next challenge to be overcome. He registered, and was accepted, to study at the medical school of the prestigious Yale University, where he worked hard for many years to complete his studies and graduate as a doctor. Today, Dr. Martin is a gynaecologist specializing in infertility problems. He is happily married to Deanna, and the young couple optimistically look forward to a bright future.

Ryan's life story is a living example of Yargo Simonidis's philosophical truth: "Happiness belongs to those who create it – not to those who search for it".

THROUGH WILLPOWER
ALONE

Two-year-old Sharon was a very pretty and high-spirited
little girl. She was always singing and dancing at home,
or playing outside with her many friends. It seemed
that there was nothing that could stop this lively,
vivacious creature. And yet, one morning, the running
around and the shouts of joy came to an abrupt end.
Sharon woke up feeling hot and clammy. Her head was
thumping, and all she wanted to do was sleep. Her arms
and legs felt as if they were heavy metal bars, pinning
her down to the bed. She could barely make her voice
heard. Noticing that she was running a very high
temperature, Sharon's mother made her drink large

quantities of water, and wiped her face with a damp cloth. But the temperature refused to go down. The family doctor came and, within the hour, Sharon was admitted to hospital.

It was almost as if the destructive Polio virus waged a special war on Sharon's natural inclinations, damaging everything that made it possible for her to run around and enjoy herself. The lower part of her body was totally paralysed. She was hardly able to breathe or speak. On the face of it, it seemed to be a life sentence. But the disease didn't injure the little girl's spirit. From the moment that the fever and fatigue began to fade away, Sharon fought against her limitations. It was as if she already knew that, one day, she would become a wheelchair sports hero and an encouraging personal example to thousands of other disabled. With all her might, Sharon constantly tried to make her legs move. But, to no avail. She continued her attempts, and never lost hope.

Her parents consulted with top specialists in Israel, and then abroad. Sharon underwent a series of surgical procedures in the years that followed, in the hope of improving her condition. The little girl spent over a year in a British hospital. Her parents thought that perhaps the British physicians would be able to help her more than their Israeli counterparts. Their hopes were dashed. There was a slight improvement, but both legs remained paralysed. It seemed as if this little girl, so full of energy, was doomed to sit in a wheelchair for the rest of her life. Sharon obstinately continued trying to walk with crutches. She was the most determined and stubborn convalescent the doctors had ever encountered. Although she got up and fell down hundreds of times, she refused to give in to her exhaustion. In spite of the bloody sores on her hands from holding the crutches, she carried on trying. Within about a year, Sharon had learned how to move around the hospital corridors on her crutches, and achieved what many had thought to be impossible.

Back in Israel to start kindergarten, she insisted that she didn't want any more doctors or operations. Her parents were very concerned about the difficulties their five-year-old daughter, hobbling on her crutches, would have to face – especially the reactions of the other children. Thanks to Sharon's nature, however, she fitted into the kindergarten very quickly. She took part in almost all the activities, just like the other children. Her excellent control over her crutches meant that she could move around from place to place. She took part in all the children's games – except jumping. When the kids played "Salt, Mustard, Vinegar, Pepper", Sharon would stand and turn the rope for her friends to skip over. At first, her friends were a little uncomfortable with the way she insisted on playing every game, but this quickly turned into admiration. The kids no longer saw her as "the girl on crutches". Instead, they began to see her as a close friend.

When she was six, Sharon transferred to an elementary school close to her home. Her father, a senior police officer and a member of the Centre's Board of

Directors, suggested that she also come to the Centre. At first, she did so a little unwillingly. However, coming three or four times a week, she learned to control the wheelchair and play games in it with the other disabled kids. She swam a lot, and began to understand that there were possibilities for her at the Centre that didn't exist outside. Her intensive activities involved great physical exertion. After every session, her muscles ached from total exhaustion, and yet she felt a wonderful uplifting of her spirit. She would return home physically exhausted, but immediately sat down to do her homework until late at night. She had a special ability to overcome her fatigue and was re-energized by her sports training.

Sharon now came to the Centre five times a week. From her many years of perseverance and gradual progress, she understood that her efforts brought reward. The muscles of her arms and shoulders had become very strong. She was able to use crutches and, later, a walking stick. At home, she demanded to be given every task she was capable of doing. She insisted on clearing the table, and helping her mother to wash the dishes. She always wanted to help her mother with the housework, and firmly refused any consideration of her physical limitations. It was difficult to ignore her vivacity, charm and pleasant nature. No one, apart from Sharon herself, realized just how much effort she had to invest in every single movement – or how difficult it was for her to do things that others did with ease. Sharon taught herself to need less sleep and to work harder in order to excel at her studies and other responsibilities. Sharon took part in a wide range of athletic activities. She swam, trained in field events, played table tennis and basketball. She was never late for a training session, and hardly ever missed one. Nor did she ever use her sports activities as an excuse to miss out on her studies or social commitments. She soon became one of the most popular, attractive and accomplished female athletes at the Centre. These positive traits became even more conspicuous when she began her studies at Tel Aviv University.

Sharon is an outstanding and versatile sportswoman, and Doubles champion in national women's wheelchair tennis. She also organizes the international wheelchair tennis tournaments in Israel on a volunteer basis. Sharon is married to Mordechai Huderland, a reputable businessman and disabled athlete, and is a devoted mother to their three daughters. She does not want to be seen as a symbol or a legend. All her achievements, in every field of life, have been achieved through her determination, perseverance and hard work – like the little ant who, with resourcefulness, wisdom and diligence is able to pick up and carry weights seven times heavier than its own body. These traits enabled Sharon to rehabilitate herself to the fullest degree.

Sharon became a highly respected lawyer and a popular member of Israeli society. She is a member of the Centre's Board of Directors. Her dedication to the Centre is great. It taught her to work hard, to persevere, and always to aspire to succeed. She has also taken part in several successful fund-raising tours to the United States, where – as well as raising funds – she has made a large number of new friends and admirers. No wonder, therefore, that a Chicago journalist named her "Wonder Woman".

***

Zippi Rubin (Rosenbaum) is one of the best known disabled female athletes in the world. She first came to the Centre as an eleven-year-old girl. Throughout her athletic career, she won dozens of world championships in field events, her major achievements being in the field of javelin throwing. From the Tokyo Paralympics in 1964 until Seoul in 1988, Zippi won seven consecutive Olympic gold medals for the javelin event.

Zippi was born in Tel Aviv's run-down Nordia neighbourhood, and absorbed her love of sports from her father, Abraham Rosenbaum, an outstanding soccer player in his day. From her father, Zippi learned not just to love sport and its intoxicating atmosphere, but also to understand the heavy price that athletes have to pay for success, and the immense efforts required, both in terms of time and physical endurance. Around the family table, there were always fascinating conversations about sports games and great moments. Everybody in the house lived for sport, and dreamt about it at night. But Zippi was denied the chance to realize her dreams. The kids in the neighbourhood simply refused to play with her. Her big crutches and wheelchair scared them. When Zippi wanted to take part in the children's activities at the local sports clubs, she was refused. Even at school, she wasn't allowed to take part in the physical education classes. Zippi went through a difficult period of depressing solitude, which made her very embittered. One day, her father told her that he had heard about a sports centre for disabled in Ramat Gan. Zippi got there as quickly as she could in her wheelchair. For the first time in her life she was made welcome at a sports club.

Zippi began to train in swimming and basketball. She was the only girl in some of these activities. Coach Streifler noted the amazing way she threw a ball. He suggested that she learn to throw the discus, shot put and javelin. Like the other members of the Centre, she trained five times a week. After two years of hard work, it became obvious that a new throwing champion had been born. Zippi was a talented basketball player as well, playing as an equal with the boys. Everything she did was for the enjoyment of taking part in sports activities – which had been denied her up until then. Now, she could also join in the conversation around the dinner table at home – about her sports achievements and her coaches, especially her field events' coach, Edna Medalia, who greatly inspired her.

Zippi's determination as an athlete could be seen in a municipal swimming event that took place in Tel Aviv. A thousand swimmers had come to take part in a five km. swim in the open sea. Zippi was among them, swimming alongside Coach Reuven Heller. The sea was high and dangerous because of a sudden fierce storm. The event organizers sent motor boats out to the open sea with megaphones, to stop the race and pick up the swimmers from the turbulent waters. Heller asked Zippi to get out, but she refused. "I'm going on", she shouted, and Heller had no choice but to respect her decision. Zippi battled courageously against the churning waves, determinedly propelling her body through the high waves. Meanwhile, a number of escort boats frantically chased after her, trying to persuade the stubborn swimmer to give up the race. Zippi stopped only when she reached the finishing point. She arrived first, at the head of a small number of fearless swimmers who had followed her lead.

Zippi is proud of the full and active life she leads. She married Arye Rubin, a disabled athlete and a world champion swimmer, who later became a swimming coach. The couple have three children, who admire their parents, and particularly the fact that their mother was elected to the Jewish Champions Hall of Fame in Israel in 1989, as the most outstanding female Jewish athlete in the world.

***

Twelve-year-old Caroline Tabib is already considered to be a veteran athlete. When she first came to the Centre at age three, her lower body was completely paralysed and her upper body was very weak, which also led to respiratory difficulties. She moved around at home, where she lived with her single mother, by crawling around on the floor. The intensive training she received at the Centre was physically and psychologically very demanding. Her mother, who accompanied her wherever she went, would stand at the edge of the swimming pool, encouraging her every move and rewarding her with hugs and kisses when she succeeded. Six months after she started training, her family doctor was very pleased with her progress, and especially the development in her upper torso and breathing. Her spirits greatly improved, and she began making friends with the other disabled children at the pool. Over the next two years, her progress continued, and she became the darling of the swimming pool. Encouraged by her achievements, she gained self-confidence, and began using a wheelchair for the first time.

When she got to elementary school, where she was the only disabled child, she aroused the other children's curiosity. Their interest soon turned to friendship. Caroline devotes many hours to her studies. Life has already taught her that she has to work much harder than other children to achieve what she wants. Her hard work at school has made her an excellent student. In spite of the fact that she is confined to a wheelchair, she is popular, and always ready to help the weaker pupils with their homework.

When she was an infant her mother used to read her stories before she went to sleep. Since 2nd Grade she has turned the tables, and insists on reading a story to her Mum every night. Caroline currently trains in the pool, wheelchair racing, wheelchair table tennis and has recently started wheelchair dancing, where she has quite quickly become one of the best dancers. She is now the cheerleader of the group.

Caroline has great charm and intelligence, and is already a successful spokeslady on the Centre's behalf. One might think that an outstanding athlete like Caroline would want a future in competitive sport but, surprisingly enough, Caroline has a different dream. When she grows up, she wants to take care of animals and study to be a vet.

***

Israela Tasma was born to a family of new immigrants from Ethiopia. She joined the Centre when she was three years old with almost total paralysis of her lower body, and considerable weakness in her upper torso. From the earliest days, she showed great ambition and talent in her efforts in the swimming pool, and gradually progressed to field events, table tennis, and wheelchair racing. The sports activities greatly improved the condition of her upper body, enabling her to control her wheelchair extremely well. She won national championships in swimming, field events, and wheelchair racing, and participated in the 1993 team to the United States.

As a 15-year old high-school student, she was awarded a computer from the Prime Minister's Fund for her excellent high-school achievements. When she saw all her class mates preparing for army service, Israela's high spirits and self-confidence led her to demand that the IDF accept her also for military service, on a volunteer basis. After much pressure and persuasion, the army agreed to recruit her, in spite of the fact that she was confined to a wheelchair. She completed her military training at a regular camp, showing great commitment and willpower. After graduating from the training camp, she was accepted to the Paratroopers Brigade, where she served as a coordinator for one of the combat units.

She completed her army service with great dedication and honour, gaining the respect and admiration of all the people who came into contact with her. Israela Tasma, with her full integration into the circles of Israeli life, symbolizes the great success of the Centre's rehabilitation mission.

UNDAUNTED

Ilan Lusky was born with muscular dystrophy, which affected his lower body, virtually paralysing both of his legs. The skinny, miserable little boy first came to the Centre when he was four years old. He was able only to crawl, and often asked his mother if he would ever be able to walk. It was in the swimming pool, full of similarly disabled children, that Ilan came to life. The sensation of effortless movement he discovered in the water allowed him to move his paralysed legs a little. He started intensive training in earnest, exercising every day. After a year of hard work, his leg muscles improved to such a degree that his mother, encouraged by this hard won development, began bringing him to the pool four times a week.

Two years after first coming to the Centre, Ilan's joy knew no bounds. He was finally able to stand up, with the help only of crutches or a walking stick. After another two years of intensive and exhausting training, he was able to walk on his own two legs – albeit with a limp, but without a crutch or even a stick to aid him. Ilan – proud of his efforts – already imagined himself dancing. But, despite his hard work, this didn't happen. His mood changed, and a feeling of mental fatigue and depression dampened his enthusiasm. He began staying at home and missing his training sessions. He would stare at the walls of his room, or thumb through a book without reading a word. He became angry and bitter – the Centre had given him such high hopes, yet he had never felt more handicapped, weak and exhausted than he did at these awful moments. He was bitterly disappointed and demoralized.

After a few weeks spent at home, Ilan found it increasingly difficult to walk – even with a stick. He felt lethargic most of the time, and his energies seemed to be draining away. A little frightened, he nevertheless tried to take a few steps. His legs gave way under him, and he fell down. He realized then that if he carried on sitting at home, doing nothing, he would sooner or later have to go back to sitting in a wheelchair. This thought was not a welcome one – especially when he realized what the other kids at the Centre would think of him. When his mother next came into his room he mumbled, with studied indifference: "You know what, Mum, maybe we'll go to the Centre tomorrow". The renewed training and routine did him good. He gradually felt his energies and enthusiasm returning. He even began training now for tennis and field events. His many activities in the field of sport gave him a feeling of confidence in his own ability to overcome obstacles and to get things done. It was the same in school. Ilan knew that perseverance and hard work would help him to improve his social status among his peers. Despite his heavy sports schedule, Ilan became an excellent student and gradually became a leading figure, influencing the other students.

Over the years, Ilan developed into an athletic young boy. He took part in local swimming and field events competitions and championships for disabled children. He even took first place in a number of them. He enjoyed the attention and admiration of his fellow athletes, his school friends and his family. In his heart, he saw himself following in the footsteps of the legendary champion, Baruch Hagai. The next sport Ilan set out to conquer was the medium and long-distance wheelchair races. At the same time, he also started playing in the wheelchair tennis league.

Ten-year-old Ilan Lusky's dream was fulfilled when, in recognition of his achievements and perseverance, he was selected to represent Israel at the Miami World Championships for Disabled Children (Junior Orange Bowl Sports Ability Games). He won gold medals in swimming and field events. His wins were not just on a personal level, but also reflected the high standard of sports activities for the disabled in Israel, in contrast to other countries. Another important achievement was on the social level – Ilan became very popular with the other athletes, and was liked by everyone. For this reason, he was awarded a trophy as "Most Outstanding Young Athlete" at these international championships.

Ilan represented Israeli sports for the disabled at its best. The smiling youth was popular with his friends, and his young and dynamic personality attracted considerable attention from the Centre's friends abroad. His command of English was good, far surpassing that of many of his peers, and he represented the Centre abroad on several occasions.

His great commitment to sport did not prevent Ilan from continuing with his economics and business administration studies. Ilan Lusky now serves as a member of the Centre's Board of Directors, representing the young disabled athletes.

***

Yeshayahu Schneller was one of the last victims of the Polio epidemic. After his release from hospital, despite the fact that both of his legs were paralysed, his parents immediately began to prepare him for his future life. His father was the headmaster of a religious school. He knew that his son would be able to lead an active life only if he was forced to deal with the realities of his disabilities. He, therefore, made Yeshayahu get up every

morning together with his older siblings. At the
beginning, the boy was able to move around the house
only by crawling. After a while, he made progress, and
was able to walk with the help of crutches and, later,
walking sticks. He loved going out to the school
playground to play games with his friends. He had fun,
leaning on his crutch or stick with one hand, and
catching and throwing balls with the other – even taking
part in games of volleyball. He was very happy, and
enjoyed being with his friends.

When Schneller was twelve, he moved with his
parents and four siblings to live near the religious
Kibbutz Yavneh, where he went to school. The open
fields of the kibbutz presented him with new challenges.
Sport, games and walks were a very important part of
the kibbutz children's lives, and almost everyone had a
bicycle. Yeshayahu's father decided to construct a
special bicycle for his son, the wheels of which could
be turned by hand. Schneller also started swimming in
the kibbutz pool. Since the swimming pool was quite a
distance from the housing units, and the path there was
full of potholes, his father organized a horse and cart to
take him to his training sessions. Long hours of
exhausting training strengthened his arm muscles and
– above all – his self-confidence. In a few short years,
Schneller persevered and was able to compete with the
best swimmers on the kibbutz. Reality taught him that
every day would bring new and difficult problems to
overcome. He learned to anticipate the battles that
awaited him, and to enjoy his sweet victories over them.

With the advance of technology, Schneller was able to use leg braces to help him to walk, leaning determinedly only on one stick, despite his paralysed legs – which meant that his other hand was free. One day, young Schneller heard from a friend about the sports centre for the disabled. But he was discouraged by what he saw there. This young kibbutznik was used to seeing ordinary youngsters around him. He was a little unsettled by the sight of so many disabled. His parents, who had come with him, reassured him: "It doesn't matter what you see", his father explained, "What is important, is what you do". Schneller followed this advice.

The two sports branches that attracted him most were swimming and table tennis. Coach Baruch Hagai accompanied him into the table tennis hall. Schneller was confident that his arms and hands were physically powerful, and he decided to have a go, and play one game. Since he was standing up, aided by a stick, he was confident that he could outplay and beat Hagai. But, using his wheelchair to "leap" from side to side, Hagai won easily. Schneller realized that modesty might have prevented his mistake, and that there was a lot he could learn. He was a conscientious and intelligent student, who enjoyed the challenge of learning new things and meeting new friends – friends very different from those at the kibbutz.

His parents, who were determined not to spoil their son, insisted that the boy get to the Centre by public transport. This meant taking the bus from the kibbutz

to the central bus station in Tel Aviv, and another bus
from there to the Centre. The journey took about two
hours in each direction. This presented Schneller with
yet another difficulty – being on the roads for four hours,
and the additional problem of getting up and down the
stairs of the bus under the probing eyes of the other
passengers. After a few years of training in three sports
branches, Schneller gave up swimming and
concentrated on table tennis and basketball. Two years
later, he won second place in the national wheelchair
table tennis championship; after another year of very
hard training, the championship was his.

He also loved basketball, and spent many hours
playing the game. He became a keen player, daring and
resourceful. He gave his all to the game and swept his
team-mates along with him. Coach Hagai, who
identified these traits, recruited Schneller to the Ramat
Gan team. Schneller urged the team on to become a
symbol of excellence, with a deep commitment to
training. He himself became the pivotal figure of the
team, proving himself to be a responsible, intelligent
and courageous player, full of energy and fighting spirit.
Schneller's participation in the national wheelchair
basketball league games meant that he had to spend
many hours on the basketball court, and additional hours
on the road. Some of the games went on until ten o'clock
at night, and it was impossible for Schneller to get back
to the kibbutz. Hagai would drive the boy to his
grandmother's home in Bnei Brak, and, very early the
next morning, Schneller would hurry off to the central

bus station in Tel Aviv to catch a bus back to the kibbutz. He always got back to school on time – without showing any signs of fatigue. He felt that he was in control of his life.

Even when he began studying at the Mercaz HaRav Yeshiva in Jerusalem, he continued to play basketball. This consumed a lot of his time, and sometimes he missed Torah studies. The head of the Yeshiva, Rabbi Zvi Yehuda Kook, who saw the intelligent student in him, never admonished him for his absences. On the contrary, the Rabbi called Schneller in for a friendly discussion, and encouraged his student not to neglect his sports activities: "In your case, sports are no less important for you than your studies". Schneller's love of sport also led him to undertake the task of volleyball referee, which was a very rewarding task for him. He began refereeing in the youth teams, and, because of his fairness and sense of justice, was nominated as volleyball referee for Israel's national league.

After completing his yeshiva high-school education with high distinction, he already knew what he wanted to do. He was competitive, tenacious, intelligent and had the ability to commit himself and work hard without counting the hours. The Law Faculty at the Bar-Ilan University was obviously the appropriate place for him, and he energetically got to grips with the studies there. Here, too, he excelled, despite his still active involvement in basketball games. At the final graduation ceremony, he was chosen to make a speech on behalf of the graduates in his clear and distinct voice.

His wisdom and integrity, together with his gentleness and calm, led many disabled athletes to consult with him – about their position on the basketball team, their relations with the coach, and even more intimate matters. Off the basketball court, and despite the fact that he was the youngest member of the team, Schneller became a kind of father figure, always ready to lend an ear to his team-mates' problems and give them his wise advice. He was also a member of several Israeli wheelchair basketball delegations to the United States, and took a leading role in games against top American basketball teams.

When the first wave of settlement in Samaria got under way, Schneller moved to Karnei Shomron together with his wife Esther. They were among the first residents, and raised their five sons there. Schneller served for many years as regional council chairman of this flourishing and developing community. His election as a member of the Centre's Board of Directors was a natural development.

After completing his studies at Bar-Ilan University, he began working for one of Israel's leading law firms. He became an accomplished lawyer and an associate partner in the firm. His hard work and professional reputation led Bar-Ilan University Law School – where he had only recently completed his studies – to invite him to lecture there, an additional task that Schneller willingly undertook.

After years of hard successful legal work, the Ministry of Justice nominated Schneller as a judge at the Magistrates Court. The demanding legal profession has great need of individuals with Schneller's judicial scholarship, integrity, abilities and determination. His willingness to devote immense energies to his work has brought him great appreciation and respect in legal circles and in the eyes of the general public. In 2004, after several years at the Magistrates Court, Schneller was promoted and appointed as judge at the Greater Tel Aviv District Court.

TRUE WINNERS

Yoav Kreim's central nervous system was severely damaged at birth. At first, it seemed as though only his arms had been affected. It later became clear that he was unable to move his legs, and he was also blind in his left eye. His parents took him from one doctor to another. Yoav himself wasn't aware of any particular problem. His mother and father were with him all the time – they carried him everywhere, and he could always feel the warmth of their bodies. His mother was a kindergarten teacher, and his father was a poet. It was almost as if his parents breathed together with him. Little Yoav felt as though they were all one living family body – in which he played a major role. When other children of his age began to walk, Yoav was barely able to crawl. His parents carried him or took him in a pushchair to his room or to the park near their home in Ramat Chen. It was only then, when he met the neighbours' children, that he realized he was different.

Other children of his age were feeding themselves, but Yoav found it hard to hold a spoon. When it slipped through his weak fingers – as it often did – he would be filled with frustration. After many repeated attempts, there was some small improvement. His parents tried to teach him to hold a ball, although this was even harder. "You'll be able to play with the other children", his father told him, and Yoav tried again and again – until he was worn out. His perseverance eventually brought success and, when he was sitting in his pushchair, Yoav could now play ball games with the neighbourhood children.

When he was three years old, his mother brought him to the Centre's kindergarten. For the first time, Yoav found himself with children who had disabilities similar to his own. He felt that he didn't belong, and didn't want to go to kindergarten. However, his parents insisted and his mother went with him to help him settle into his new environment. Once he learned how to use a walker, he was able to stand on his own two feet. This progress filled him with great joy, and he finally began to make friends with the other disabled children.

Coach Margalit Zonnenfeld took him under her wing. At first, the lack of mobility in Yoav's legs and the partial paralysis of his arms made it very difficult for him. He was scared of the water, and his progress was very slow. But the sight of the other disabled kids, who were able to swim despite similar disabilities, made him hope that he, too, would be able to do so. After several months of hard training, he was able to float, and even to move his arms and body a little in the water, and make some progress. After a year's training, he could slowly swim a length or even two of the swimming pool. He saw his ability to swim as a triumph, and derived great self-confidence from his achievements.

Yoav began studying at ILAN's "Ha-On" school for severely disabled children. He found it very difficult, during the lessons, to absorb words and letters. He tried to follow his teachers' every word, and to commit them to memory. At home, he would go over in his head everything he had learned in school, and would sit studying until late in the evening. He was deeply saddened by the learning problems he had at school. One day, Yoav was staring at the long line of letters the teacher was writing on the board. They just didn't seem to join up into words. When the teacher asked him what she had written, he looked at her in alarm. All the other kids eagerly put up their hands to answer, but all Yoav could do was to fumble with the pencil in his hand as if it would save him from disgrace. The pencil fell from his trembling fingers. Overcome by frustration, he threw himself from his seat and tumbled in shame onto the floor. He hated everybody and despised himself. He started screaming, knocking chairs over, kicking and hitting everything in sight. Sobbing, he crawled towards the door in a desperate attempt to escape from the many alarmed eyes – that followed him out into the corridor. Two of the teachers managed to get hold of him, and one of the women stroked his hair. The woman's touch comforted him. One or two frightened and wide-eyed children helped him to get up. He was mortified by what he had done, and wished he could just disappear.

That night, Yoav had a dream. He was standing on his own two feet, taking off his pyjamas and getting dressed. Nobody was helping him. He was doing up the buttons of his shirt without any difficulty, and lacing his shoes all by himself. Afterwards, he went out into the hallway and walked downstairs, without a wheelchair or crutches. He was walking! He felt so strong and proud! His cries of joy woke him from his wonderful dream. From the depths of the misery that now washed over him, Yoav realized that sport was something he could feel proud of. He began training in wheelchair table tennis and tennis. His weak arms made it hard for him to manoeuvre his wheelchair. Long months of training helped him improve his control. He found it difficult to curb his desire for competition, even in the training sessions. For Yoav, competition was a means of displaying his ability and success. He never acknowledged defeat. He always wanted first place and, if he didn't succeed, he was sure that he hadn't worked hard enough. He became a sports addict.

His many years of hard work began to bring results – second or third places in swimming or table tennis competitions. Then, finally, the top – the exhilarating experience of winning first place in the disabled children's table tennis and swimming championships. He felt that he was at last realizing his dreams. His sports activities also opened up his social life. Most of his friends now were disabled athletes he had come to know from training sessions and competitions. Sports had made him popular, always surrounded by friends.

As the years went by, Yoav also began to make good progress in his studies. His problems with reading continued, but he learned to overcome them by concentrating on what was being said, and noting down everything he heard in class. Now he wanted to move on – to a school for non-disabled children. But no school was prepared to accept him. The head teachers claimed that the classrooms and bathrooms were not accessible to such a severely disabled boy. Their refusal to accept him hurt him deeply. In the end, he was accepted at the Ramat Chen elementary school, in combination with his continued attendance at the special "Ha-On" school for disabled children. After three years, Yoav completed elementary school. Diagnostic testing eventually revealed dyslexia, which explained his serious reading problems.

The response to his applications to high schools was generally, again, an insulting and shameful refusal to enrol disabled children. But Yoav was well schooled in the art of perseverance, and he continued his efforts. He knew that persistence would eventually win the day. And this was, indeed, the case. The head teacher of the "Tichon Chadash" high school in Tel Aviv agreed to enrol him. While grateful, Yoav knew that fresh hurdles awaited him – not just to integrate into a new school, but also – in spite of his reading difficulties – to develop his memory and become a top pupil.

Just as Yoav started his studies at the new school, his father passed away. At the time of his death, his father had been the editor of a prestigious literary journal. It was a terrible blow for Yoav, who admired his father's innovative spirit and captivating personality. He gradually recovered from his grief, and began working with even more diligence and commitment. He divided his time between sports and studies, and his days ended very late at night. His sports achievements earned him a place on the disabled children's team to the Miami World Championships for Disabled Children and Youth. At these Games, Yoav won gold medals for swimming and also for field events.

Sports alone didn't satisfy Yoav's ambitions. After completing high school, he studied hard at the Beit Berl College for his social work degree. Then, with his studies behind him, he began practical work with the disabled at the Centre. He quickly advanced to become a spokesman for the national disabled movement in Israel. Despite his speech impediments, his message is sharp and clear. Yoav demands equality and rights for the disabled. He continues to hold this position, and his success as a social affairs commentator and public leader is recognized and appreciated by all sectors of the Israeli public.

**

Mate Mazor, now aged seventeen, emigrated from Argentina with his family when he was six years old. He was completely paralysed in both legs, partially paralysed in both arms, his speech was impaired and he was deeply depressed about his condition. His parents, who were unable to find an adequate rehab centre in Argentina, decided to come to Israel and get the best possible treatment for Mate. Eleven years of experience at the ISCD have proved that they made the right move. Mate's condition, and especially his psychological state, has changed dramatically. The paralysis in his arms has slightly diminished, and the muscles of his upper body have been strengthened.

These changes came about only gradually, as a result of Mate's very intensive training programme, which made great demands on his physical and mental energies. Above all, these physical changes and Mate's tremendous determination and resolve have boosted his self-confidence and improved his ability to speak. He is no longer the helpless child he once was. In spite of the huge amounts of time and energy he expends at the Centre, Mate also reserves energy for his school studies, and is an outstanding pupil.

These great changes have also improved Mate's ability to cope with the difficulties he faces with every waking moment. Each movement he makes requires incredible physical exertion and willpower. Mate has learned from his sports activities how to cope with these obstacles more successfully. He also understands that his progress and achievements at school and at the

Centre, the main interest around which his young life revolves, can only be advanced by maximum effort. Today, Mate is a superb student with tremendous self-confidence. He is charismatic, outgoing and one of the best examples of how the Centre helps turn children from helplessness towards integration into Israeli life. Mate continues to focus his energies on wheelchair racing, swimming and table tennis. In his short career as an athlete, he has already set a number of youth world records in wheelchair racing, swimming and field events at the Miami Games for Disabled Children.

Mate says with pride that the Centre has changed his life. So, what does a youngster with such serious disabilities have to say about his future? "I will work harder and longer hours to succeed in sports and in life. One day I hope to be Director of the Israel Sport Centre for the Disabled", says Mate enthusiastically. "This way, I will able to help many disabled children like myself".

***

In the first years of the new millennium, young CP-disabled swimmer, Itzik Mamistavlov, began to become known in the international sports arena. Mamistavlov came to the Centre as a three-year-old. Already at the age of five, he began to show outstanding qualities as a swimmer and, after a few years, became the disabled children's swimming champion. At the 2002 world swimming championships in Argentina, he won a gold medal for 50 m. freestyle, and a silver medal for 100

m. freestyle. Mamistavlov made great progress in 2004,
at the Athens Paralympics, when he won two Olympic
gold medals, for 50 m. and 100 m. freestyle. In 2007
his accomplishments soared, when he won three gold
medals for 50 m., 100 m. and 200 m. freestyle, breaking
a world record. This talented young athlete continues
to bring great pride and recognition to the State of Israel.

**

Two additional new young talents followed in
Mamistavlov's footsteps, and made their mark at the
end of the first decade of the new millennium. Both
Roman Chudin, who immigrated to Israel from Russia,
and Israeli-born Danny Bovrov, are also very severely
disabled. They have amazed the disabled sports
community in Israel with their outstanding talents
playing table tennis. After their successes in the Israeli
National Championships, the two are set on competing
in the international arena, and then the 2012 London
Paralympic Games.

THE STRUGGLE FOR
SELF-ESTEEM

Mariel Arbutman was a very premature baby. He was placed in an incubator immediately after his birth in Riga, in the former Soviet Union. His parents, Pesia and Alexander, noticed that he was very still and that his cries were feeble. Thinking that this was normal for such a premature baby, they weren't alarmed. When they came to take Mariel home from the hospital, however, the doctor asked to speak to them. He told them that the infant's brain had been damaged due to an insufficient oxygen supply in the incubator. As a result, he was paralysed in both arms and both legs. His parents were stunned. After overcoming their initial shock, they told the doctor that they had every hope that, with physiotherapy, they could improve their son's condition. The doctor's response was noncommittal.

The Arbutmans looked after their son devotedly, treating him in shifts. They brought him to a physiotherapist three times a day. They hoped that this regimen would improve their son's condition. Pesia, who was a nurse by profession, soon also sensed that her son wasn't crying normally. She brought him back to the hospital for additional tests. A week later, Mariel's parents received an additional blow. The doctors told them that their infant son was also deaf and dumb. The Arbutmans refused to come to terms with this harsh news, and added speech therapy to their son's routine.

Mariel was six when the family immigrated to Israel. The normal difficulties of integration into a new country were compounded by the problems inherent in bringing up a child with such devastating disabilities. Mariel's parents sought a suitable framework for their son. When six-year-old Mariel first came to the Centre, in his unwieldy wheelchair, he was bewildered. He had never seen sports facilities or a swimming pool before. His eyes lit up. He saw hundreds of disabled kids around him. His lips moved, reflecting his excitement.

When Mariel started learning to swim, it took two coaches and his father – who was his constant companion – to carry him into the pool, and to calm him down. At first, the child simply lay on top of the water, supported by the two coaches, so that he wouldn't sink. Once he got used to this new experience, he began moving his head from side to side. This was the only part of his body that Mariel could move. His coaches thought that the best method would be for him to swim on his back, by tenaciously and persistently moving his head from side to side – like a propeller. After a gruelling six years of training, four times a week, Mariel very slowly succeeded in swimming the 12.5 metre width of the pool. It took him about fifteen minutes. The condition of one of his paralysed legs now also improved slightly as a result of his hard work, and he was able to move it a little.

Mariel was a very ambitious and determined child. His swimming activities were no longer enough for him. He had discovered what he was able to achieve in the water using just his head movements. Now he wanted to use this ability out of the water as well. He started watching the disabled children playing table tennis in their wheelchairs. One day, while watching, Mariel moved his electric wheelchair close to the table, bent his head down and caught the ping-pong ball in his mouth. With a swift jerk of his head, he managed to throw the ball to the player at the other side of the table. This episode opened a new chapter of his life.

Mariel tried holding the table tennis racket in his mouth. He trained hard despite experiencing many moments of failure and despair. He would often return home in an edgy and agitated state, and would angrily bang his head against the wall or the cupboard. Since he was unable to speak, this was the only way he could express his disappointment and frustration. His parents would soothe him, and he would be back training the following day as if nothing had happened. Very gradually, his efforts bore fruit. After about a year, he was able to play a game – and he was the happiest person alive. His roars of happiness filled the Arbutman home.

When Mariel was fourteen, he began playing tennis. After many exhausting training sessions, he succeeded in holding the heavy tennis racket in his mouth. The racket had a specially adapted handle, and a brace was fitted into his mouth to support his jaw while he played. Mariel's athletic achievements greatly encouraged him in his ambition to become more independent. Although, on the face of it, his achievements seemed so few, in his eyes – and in the eyes of everyone around him – they were incredible. He began using his mouth and teeth as if they were his hands. He turned taps on, and then lowered his head to drink from them. He took food from the table, or even leafed through the newspaper or a book – all with his mouth alone. Mariel learned that, through sports activities, he had acquired the capability to do things that nobody had believed possible. In recent years, to fill his many hours of free time and fulfil his need for creativity, Mariel has even become quite an accomplished artist – holding the paintbrush in his mouth.

His persistence and self-discipline, and his unique ability to overcome frustration and despair, have made Mariel a familiar figure at the Sports Centre. Despite his impaired speech, he succeeds in communicating through head movements, and the special sounds he is able to make with his mouth. He always conveys the same message – "Never give up!"

Mariel will never be able to move his arms and legs, and he will always be a deaf mute, but he has become a proud athlete, admired for his incredible efforts by everyone around him. It is almost as if he was reborn, with diminished physical disabilities. Through the Centre, Mariel has enjoyed many happy moments. Such a moment was when he was nominated Rehab Sports Hero. Another such moment for Mariel was when he played an exhibition table tennis game with Prime Minister Ehud Olmert, during the latter's visit to the Centre. Olmert, a keen athlete and sports fan, was visibly moved and amazed by his opponent's special skills and spirit.

Mariel Arbutman's life presents a particularly poignant moral dilemma. Today, the issue of whether or not a pregnancy should be terminated when prenatal testing detects severe deformities in the embryo is being questioned. In other words, given the option, should society allow the birth of a baby with devastating disabilities.

Israeli Chief Rabbi, Meir Lau, who is also chairman of the Yad Vashem Council, regards this as a kind of "selection process" over the right to live or die – with the attendant memories of the barbaric Nazi regime. Chief Rabbi Lau believes that only when the mother's life is endangered is it permissible – from a halakhic point of view – to terminate a pregnancy. In Mariel's case, it is clear that the optimistic environment of the Centre and the satisfaction he derives from his limited sports achievements are only one side of the coin. Despite Mariel's sports capabilities, he still has to lead a very sheltered and non-independent life.

FROM A VICTIM TO A WINNER

Baruch Massami was born with two short stumps instead of legs. One of his arms was also badly deformed and almost completely paralysed. After his birth, his parents worried that he would frighten his eight siblings, especially as the whole family lived crowded together in a small, dilapidated two-roomed flat. His despairing mother eventually decided to leave him in the hospital.

The first few weeks of the infant's life were spent undergoing a battery of medical tests, to determine the reason for his disabilities. Once the tests were completed, the doctors began wondering what could be done for such a helpless, deformed child. From the contacts with his parents, it was clear that it would be impossible for them to accommodate such a severely disabled child in their tiny flat. He was transferred from one hospital to another, where kind-hearted nurses tended to his needs. When he reached the age when normal children get down from the bed and out of nappies, the doctors decided to move him to the ALYN Children's Rehabilitation Hospital in Jerusalem. Here he learned how to crawl on the floor, and to move around on his stumps. Baruch was undemanding, and cooperated with his caretakers. Everyone called him by his surname – Massami.

When he was four and a half, his parents were persuaded to take their son home. All that awaited him there was a small bed that had been crammed into one of the two tiny rooms. Massami cowered on the bed, terrified. His new environment scared him. After a while, he managed to slide off the bed, and, using his arms, quickly wriggled forward like a lizard. His brothers and sisters were repulsed. He looked to them like some disgusting creature, who would make their already hard life even harder. Little Massami sensed that he wasn't wanted. He sat on the floor, curled up into himself, humiliated and hurt. To him everyone looked like giants, as he hopped around by their feet. He spent his first night at home fighting tears. He didn't want anyone to hear him crying.

Massami's unschooled parents were so busy putting bread on the family table that they had little time for him. His mother left home early in the morning for her job as a cleaner, and returned, exhausted, in the evening. His embittered and despairing father was an alcoholic of long standing. Parents like these were unable to help this child. They didn't even realize that they could contact the health authorities to obtain a wheelchair for him. Massami felt like a prisoner in the small flat. He soon began crawling around, jumping and hopping about like a frog in the house, the garden and even in the street. His wretched appearance scared all the neighbours, who avoided him. Young Massami was bewildered and hurt by the horror that seemed to take hold of people when they saw him.

His family was embarrassed by him. When his brothers' and sisters' friends came to the small flat, he was made to feel unwelcome. They made it quite clear to him that he was supposed to disappear, and not scare the guests away. He became used to a solitary life. He didn't sit at the table with the rest of the family. He would sit on the other side of the room and eat on the floor – and felt relieved when nobody glared at him in astonishment and disgust.

Massami enrolled at the kindergarten near his home. At first, the other kids were terrified, and ran away from him. Then they began to call him names, and even to kick him. He lay on the floor, completely helpless to defend himself. Once, after the hysterical children had almost trampled him, Massami suddenly shook himself free, and began to scream and howl, like a wounded, crazed animal. The children ran away in terror. The kindergarten teacher did her best to shield him, but her efforts were in vain. After two days of abuse and humiliation, Massami hopped off on his stumps, and escaped from the kindergarten. He found refuge nearby, in a large, empty park. He sat there on the grass and cried his eyes out. His teacher, accompanied by the other children, followed the sounds of his weeping until she found him. She went up to him and stroked his head. The children around him bowed their heads in shame. Their relationship with him improved from that day on. Massami realized that he, too, would have to do something to make the other kids like him. He began playing with them, and made huge efforts to hop everywhere on his stumps, and to catch the balls – even if one of his hands was very deformed. He put a smile on his face, even when he was in great pain. His efforts to join in the other kids' games were so tiring that he would fall into bed after getting home, completely worn out.

When he began elementary school, nobody wanted to sit next to him in the classroom. A disabled relative, who heard about his problems, gave him an old, adult-sized wheelchair. Massami was almost lost inside it, but it did made it easier for his mother to take him to school. Seeing him sitting up high in the wheelchair, the other pupils mocked him less.

A new, embarrassing problem arose at school. Massami found reading and numbers very difficult. The letters and numbers floated in front of his eyes without any apparent order. The other kids soon caught on to the fact that he had no idea what the teacher was writing on the board, and he got the reputation of being simpleminded. In fact, Massami tried much harder than any other pupil. He sat long hours with his books after school, being helped by the neighbouring children. It was hard for him to keep up, and he was the weakest pupil in the class. He moved up from year to year largely because the teachers were considerate of his condition. The contempt of his classmates began to grow, and they even started hitting him. They saw him as a cripple, in body and mind. He didn't take part in the class trips, and he wasn't invited to any of the parties. All the kids made fun of him. At the same time, the misery at home increased. His father died from a liver disease brought on by alcoholism. His embittered and worn-out mother began beating him and reviling him for his failures at school. He felt unloved and unwanted. He didn't believe that anything good could ever happen to him.

Massami thoughts were gloomy, and people around him kept their distance. Since he studied in a religious school, he tried to believe in God, and prayed to God to help him. But it seemed to him that even God was spurning and ignoring him. And then, one day, one of the teachers volunteered to give him private lessons in reading and arithmetic. Massami found this offer difficult to believe, but he gratefully accepted it. This teacher, in fact, developed a special method to help him. He would put a ruler over the writing on the lines below the line where Massami was reading, so that he wouldn't be confused – and the method worked.

When Massami was ten years old, he was invited to the Beit Levenstein Hospital to be fitted with prostheses.

He spent three months in the hospital, learning how to fit the prostheses onto his two short stumps, and how to harness them to his body with strong leather straps. His first steps were faltering and scared him. After many hours of exercise, however, he was able to take a few steps – albeit with great difficulty. The prostheses rubbed, and caused big sores on his stumps. Despite the pain, he persevered with the prostheses – especially for going to school. He felt as though his head was in the clouds, and this wonderful feeling gave him pride and self-confidence. The other pupils were surprised to see him standing. They suddenly saw him in a different light. Gone were the defeated face and the downcast eyes; in their place was a tall, dark-haired youth with determined features and an aquiline nose. He began to make friends. The prostheses continued to cut into his stumps, but Massami refused to take them off at school, even when the pain was unbearable. He preferred to walk slowly and painfully with his prostheses, than to face ridicule and humiliation. Only when he was sitting at home did he permit himself, with relief, to take them off and give his wounded stumps a respite from the pain and inflammation.

At junior high school, Massami started taking part in the physical education classes. Despite the feeling that his stumps were getting more and more torn with every move he made, he would not give up. He did things that didn't require a lot of movement. He usually played handball games or took the position of goalkeeper, developing amazing side leaps for this purpose. His days as a crawling infant, when he had used his hands as a replacement for his legs, helped him to fall properly and with resilience onto the ground. His success in catching the ball raised his prestige in the eyes of the other kids. Despite his improved social status, his studies once again took a turn for the worse.

The educational authorities decided to send him for psychological re-evaluation. From the results of the tests, it became evident that Massami was not psychologically abnormal. However, he did have an additional, so far undiagnosed, disability – the boy was dyslexic. He simply didn't function normally as far as reading and writing were concerned. Massami now found himself in the hands of an educational therapist. It was she who told him about the sports centre for the disabled in Ramat Gan. The therapist also showed him newspaper clippings of disabled Israeli athletes in wheelchairs, taking part in the Paralympics, including a photo of Baruch Hagai. Massami sniggered derisively, as if he didn't believe a word she was saying.

At this same time, Massami had an enormous crush on a girl at school, and his feelings were reciprocated. For the first time in his life, he was filled with happiness and hope. When he visited his girlfriend's home, however, he was met by her parents' sour looks. "You can leave right now", her father contemptuously told him. "And don't come near my daughter again. Do you hear me? You miserable cripple!" And that was the end of Massami's brief romance.

Once again, Massami began to react violently

whenever he was upset. Even an annoying glance in his direction could set off an outburst of anger. Not a day passed without blows and brawls. He caused a great deal of damage and destruction. The other pupils put as much distance as possible between themselves and him. Massami decided to pay the whole world back for the insults he had received. Because of his outbursts, he was asked to leave school when he was just fifteen. "He should be in a criminal institution", angrily blurted one of the teachers – but this time Massami wasn't at all offended. He felt relieved that wouldn't have to go to school any longer. He shut himself away at home, and snapped back angrily at his mother's questions. And yet, the situation still bothered him. He began to turn over in his mind what the educational therapist had told him about the sports centre for disabled. When his oldest brother came home, Massami put his thoughts into words, "How do you feel about taking me to the sports centre for the disabled? Maybe I'll be able to do something there". His brother responded favourably.

When fifteen-year-old Massami first came to the Centre, Coach Reuven Heller was stirred by his severe disabilities, and took the new trainee under his wing. The first thing Coach Heller did was to seat him in one of the specially adapted sports wheelchairs. Massami was very moved by the fact that Heller was going to so much effort for him. He rode around the Centre's paths in the wheelchair, and began to feel a little more relaxed.

Heller now urged Massami to learn how to control and manoeuvre the wheelchair. Later on, he also encouraged him to join the swimming sessions, as well as weightlifting. Massami was greatly excited and encouraged by the fact that people were taking such an interest in what he was doing, and he began to pay attention to what was going on around him. Coach Heller took advantage of this awakening interest to motivate Massami to take part in other fields of sport. His progress also brought him the attention of the other coaches and disabled athletes.

Massami began to practise racing every day in his own neighbourhood. Speeding along in his wheelchair, he caught the attention of the local residents, who began chatting with him and expressing their admiration for his resolve and determination. He gradually started to make new neighbourhood friends. He was very happy with this new situation, and began to feel that, with his new mobility in the wheelchair, he could get anywhere he wanted.

He began coming to the Centre four times a week. At this stage, the weightlifting coach, Abraham Bruner, as well as the wheelchair racing coach, Dr. Shayke Hutzler, who later became the Centre's scientific adviser, also saw Massami's potential. Coach Bruner began to plant the hope in Massami's heart that if he persevered and trained hard enough, he could one day become a champion. This possibility fired Massami with enthusiasm. He saw it as a compensation for his past years of mental anguish. He wanted so much to command respect in at least one area of his life. He now came to the Centre five times a week, racing there on his wheelchair – a distance of 15 miles – as a warm-up to his training session. His bitterness gradually faded away, and he became alert and friendly and more communicative to people around him.

Massami started a course of professional training as a mechanic. This enabled him to earn his own living. His dyslexia prevented him from undertaking theoretical studies, but he was happy doing manual work. He successfully qualified, and afterwards found himself a job working in a factory that manufactured plastic components. However, his real world was one of sports. His two years of hard work bore fruit. Based on his sports merits, he was included in the Centre's delegation of young athletes to the Miami World Championships for Disabled Children and Youth. His family began to be more supportive, and his relations with them became warmer. He was the first member of the family to travel outside Israel, and everybody in his neighbourhood was proud for him.

Massami was determined to come back from Miami a winner. He would get up at four o'clock in the morning, and race in his wheelchair for several hours. He was now coming to the Centre five times a week after work, training for 3-4 hours each day. These arduous training sessions caused tremendous pain in his shoulders and other parts of his body. His hands were sore and bleeding from turning the wheels of his wheelchair. But he didn't stop training. The pains he experienced were sweet in comparison to the humiliation he had suffered in the past.

At Miami, Massami won the world championship title for Youth Wheelchair Racing. As the gold medal was presented to him, he burst into tears – this time not from humiliation. He felt as though he had been reborn. During the concluding ceremony of the Championships, he was introduced to Sarah, a twelve-year-old American athlete. Sarah was a four-limb amputee with no arms or legs. Massami was deeply shocked by her terrible mutilations; all he wanted to do was to escape from this deformed creature in the wheelchair.

"Hi", Sarah sweetly murmured. And then there was quite a lengthy silence.

Massami saw his whole lonely life flashing in front of him. He remembered the terrible life of his past – the scorn, the fear, the humiliations and the disgust that were clearly reflected in the people around him. Sarah was a little girl, looking for friendship and recognition – just like him.

Massami approached her in his wheelchair, and warmly grasped the stump of her arm. She smiled at him, very excited and happy at the attention this new young world champion was paying her.

"Would you like a coke?" Massami asked, with a broad grin on his face.

"Of course", she whispered with an admiring smile.

To this day, Massami remembers his meeting with Sarah even more vividly than the medal presentation.

ON EXCELLENCE ALONE

Complications at birth left Boaz Kramer paralysed in both legs and his left arm. Despite these disabilities, his life in the village of Ben Shemen was relatively ordinary. The kids at the village nursery school accepted Boaz, who crawled or walked awkwardly with crutches. Despite this, Boaz always felt that the other kids were being nice to him only because their parents had told them to. He tried hard to be friendly and helpful to everyone around him, and made an effort to join in all the games. He learned to move around on his crutches or in his wheelchair. Boaz tried so hard to succeed that he often fell over. He even broke his healthy arm on one occasion. But this kind of mishap didn't stop him from his constant efforts to deny his physical disability.

Simi, his mother, a nurse at the Tel Hashomer Hospital, and his father Emanuel, a scientist at the Weizmann Institute, hired a private coach, who taught him to swim in the village pool. Boaz had a musical ear, and his parents responded positively to his request to learn to play the piano. They liked his great ambition to excel. He was the best pupil in the nursery school, and would astonish everyone with his ability in arithmetic and reading. Boaz wanted people to be impressed by his abilities. When he came to swim in the village swimming pool, however, it was difficult for people to ignore his physical disabilities. At those moments, Boaz felt that whatever he did, and however good he might be, everyone would always think of his limitations rather than his abilities. He felt bitter about it. When that happened, he would sit at the piano and play, with great talent and emotion. The wonderful tunes seemed to spirit his damaged and unwieldy body away to another world – a magical, marvellous world.

When Boaz first came to the Centre's pool, at his mother's suggestion, the hectic activity around the pool scared him. Coach Margalit Zonnenfeld, who was used to this kind of response, introduced him to some of the more active kids. His mother urged him in the direction of the water, and the coach carried him in her arms into the pool. He soon felt comfortable in the water. The children around him were competitive, and measured him up by the speed of his swimming, which – compared to theirs – was still quite slow.

Boaz began to work with Coach Zonnenfeld on developing swimming techniques. He trained hard and felt that his arms were gradually gaining strength. More than anything else, he was thrilled that he was able to swim faster. Swimmers who had beaten him by five or six metres only a few months before, now beat him by only two or three metres. Boaz hoped that he would soon be able to match his sports rivals and even win. After a year or so of intensive training, he began taking part in swimming competitions. His first achievements were modest, though he was no longer the last one at the finishing line.

Even though he was very involved in the world of sport, Boaz never forgot to do his school homework. He constantly strove to be top of the class. He wanted to be judged on excellence alone. If other kids had problems in arithmetic – Boaz volunteered to help them. If there was someone who found Hebrew difficult – Boaz would come to his aid. When an editor for the school newspaper was needed – Boaz undertook the task. When an events committee was chosen to decorate the classroom – Boaz was one of the members. No other pupil put so much effort and energies into communal and school activity. Boaz felt that his efforts to stand out as a result of his achievements and commitment were being crowned with success.

And then, suddenly, his father died. Boaz felt as if he had lost one of the most important props of his life. He was frightened. He felt alone in the world, vulnerable and abandoned. He became introverted, wrapped in a solitude that drew all desire out of him. He also stopped his sports activities. After a long period of grief, Boaz returned to a gruelling schedule of training, hoping that hard work would help him forget his great loss. He now began training also in tennis. His talent and athletic abilities impressed Coach Ayelet Ringold. Her encouragement motivated him to train on a regular basis – and also to participate in competitions. He signed up for every tennis tournament and every swimming championship. His participation filled him with excitement and fulfilment. Although he would be disappointed and irritable if he took second or third place, his failure motivated him to try ever harder.

The village kids played a lot of basketball. Although in a wheelchair, Boaz also wanted to join in the game. His performance on the court was less than impressive; he couldn't even get the ball high enough to get it into the basket. This upset him. He decided to try playing basketball at the Centre. Immediately after he finished school, Boaz would come to the Centre, and spend two or three hours at a time, throwing balls at the basket. His throws were weak, especially as he threw with only one arm, and he found it very painful. The coaches kept an eye on his feeble attempts, and advised him to use a smaller and lighter ball. Boaz refused. In his mind's eye, he could see every ball he threw going through the hoop. When his vision didn't materialize, he was sure that the next time it would. Even after missing many hundreds of shots, he didn't lose faith in his ultimate success. After about a year, his wish finally came true. He succeeded in getting a ball through the hoop. Only when he was convinced that he was good enough, did Boaz start playing basketball with the Centre's team. After a year's hard work, he began to stand out as a talented and intelligent player with leadership and playing skills. He undertook the task of playmaker. After filling this position, he also became a member of the Centre's top youth wheelchair basketball team, under Coach Eli Hauben.

There were times when he thought that perhaps he should give up the exhausting training, and concentrate only on his studies. His keenest desire was to be a doctor, although he realized that his disabilities would make it difficult. When he stopped training, however, it had a bad effect on his state of mind, and he became tired, irritable and miserable. Boaz quickly returned to his training. The world of sport energized him anew. He took an interest in many of the sports competitions, and discussed them with his friends. He constantly browsed through the sports pages in the newspapers. In his eyes, sport was the most dynamic and rewarding endeavour in the world.

Boaz now began winning gold medals in the youth swimming and tennis championships. He won first place in the Rosenzweig Family Disabled Children's Swimming Championships for 50-metre crawl, 50-metre backstroke, and 50-metre freestyle. That same year, he also won tennis and table-tennis championships for disabled youth. When he returned home after the competitions, he was so exhausted and tired that he couldn't get to sleep. At these times, he would sit by the piano and play delightful, tender melodies that revitalized him and brought him peace of mind, as well as courage and hope to face the hard days ahead.

After five years of intensive training, Boaz was chosen to represent the Centre at the Miami World Championships for Disabled Children. He was filled with anticipation and excitement at the thought of competing in an international event. All his thoughts were focused on winning a medal. The morning of the competition, Boaz got up early. Unable to eat or drink, he waited impatiently in his room to leave for the competition site. When he got there, he hastily undressed and got into the pool to check the water temperature. He observed his surroundings and the other athletes who were warming up in the water. He particularly scrutinized the jumping-off points and the finishing line. His entire being was now focused on these two points, between which he imagined himself gliding at great speed. His arms seemed to grow longer and stronger, as he sliced through the water. He could already hear the applause of the large crowd, and the shouted encouragement of his coach. Every second before the starting shot seemed like an eternity to him. When, finally, the shot was heard, it was as if a spring quickly uncoiled within him.

Boaz won three gold medals at Miami: for crawl, backstroke and breaststroke – an exhilarating reward for years of perseverance and sheer hard work. But Boaz wasn't satisfied yet. His thoughts had already soared in the direction of the Paralympics, where he could bring glory to the State of Israel. He imagined the crowds cheering on the exhausted sports heroes in their extraordinary efforts, to overcome not merely obstacles of distance, time and height, but also, and most of all, the physical limitations that fate had dealt them. In the years that followed, Boaz concentrated on tennis. He represented Israel in a number of important international competitions, becoming an outstanding player.

Sports did much to strengthen Boaz's latent potential: helping him to develop determination, perseverance, and the ability to function under pressure. These qualities greatly helped him in his medical studies at Tel Aviv University. Boaz saw in medicine the expression of his ambition and will to contribute to society – and to be appreciated by society – in spite of his physical limitations.

Fifteen years after winning a gold medal for swimming in the Miami World Championships for Disabled Children, Boaz won a silver medal for tennis at the Beijing Paralympics. A no less important achievement was the completion of his medical studies at Tel Aviv University's Medical School. These developments proved Boaz's mettle and his supreme determination to achieve his objectives. Now, Boaz needed to decide what his next way station in life would be, as an adult. As a seriously disabled individual, he felt that the new generation of disabled children, in their thousands, needed him as a role model. In spite of his severe disabilities, he had reached the pinnacle of success. Despite the efforts and long hours he had invested in his medical training, he felt that his heart belonged to the Centre. Working on behalf of the Centre, and embracing its social and rehabilitative ideals, was what he really wanted to do with his life. As he hoped, his request to become part of the Centre's administrative staff was met with great joy and appreciation. The Centre needs people like Boaz in order to help shape the future lives of the disabled children.

IV

IN THE PATHS OF
BENEVOLENCE

Following World War II, U.S. President Harry Truman appointed Bella
Spewack as American representative to the U.N. Rehabilitation Agency for
Refugee Children. From left to right: Bella Spewack, President Harry Truman,
Sam Spewack.
(Photo courtesy Theater Arts Collection of Columbia University's Book and Manuscript
Library ([Photograph: Talbot Studios, New York])

The cornerstone-laying ceremony of the first sport centre for the disabled in
Israel. From right to left: Sam Spewack, Bella Spewack, Betty Dubiner, Arieh
Posek.
(Photo courtesy Betty Dubiner Collection [Photograph Yitzhak Berez])

Disabled children in Israel – before suitable wheelchairs were obtained for them.

Twenty-five years later – improved facilities and wheelchairs for the disabled children, in the new building funded by Michael Simmons of London.
(Photograph: Michael Freidin)

The first years – the spirit of the ISCD.
(Photograph: Alexander Ziskind)

A presidential visit. From left to right: Moshe Rashkes, President of Israel,
Prof. Ephraim Katzir, Dali Rechter, Yariv Oren, Leah Rapaport.
(Photograph: Alexander Ziskind)

The opening ceremony of the 1968 Paralympics in Jerusalem. The Israeli wheel-chair basketball team, which later won a Paralympic gold medal.
(Photograph: Yitzhak Freidin)

Captain of the Israeli team to the 1968 Paralympics, Zvi Ben-Zvi, taking the Olympic oath. Standing at his side – Coach Reuven Heller.
(Photograph: Yitzhak Freidin)

The opening ceremony of the 1968 Paralympics in Israel. Leading the parade, Gershon Huberman of Israel (right) and Charles Atkinson of England (left).

Medals from Minister of Defence Moshe Dayan, after the final game at the Centre between Israel and the United States. Standing behind, from right to left: Arieh Fink, Sir Ludwig Guttman.
(Photograph: M. Dekel)

Wheelchair tennis novices in action.
(Photograph: Michael Freidin)

President Yitzhak Navon at the Centre.
(Photograph: Alexander Ziskind)

Working to promote sports for the disabled. Michael Simmons greeting Dr. Henry Kissinger, U.S. Secretary of State.

Murray Goldman (left), sponsor of the Israeli delegation to the 1976 Toronto Paralympics, congratulating the Israeli women's wheelchair basketball gold medallists.
(Photograph: Alexander Ziskind)

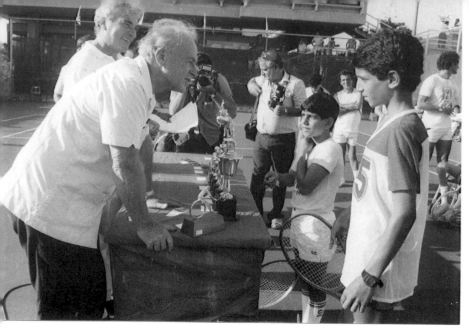

Prime Minister Yitzhak Rabin, at the Israel international wheelchair tennis championships, greeting the Centre's tennis players. Standing to his left, Dr. Ian Froman, president of the Israel Tennis Centre.

Triumph at the Miami World Championships for Disabled Children: Ilan Lusky (centre), world swimming champion.

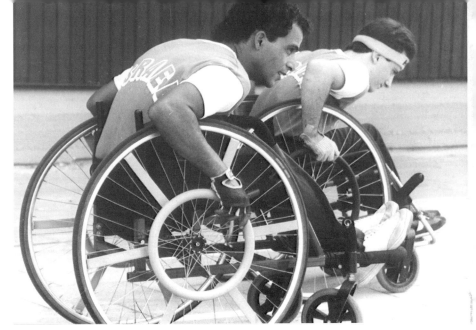

Wheelchair marathon – Ezra Elisha (left) and Shlomo Sharoni.
(Photograph: Michael Freidin)

Eyal Shertov (right) playing basketball against the visiting Dutch team.
(Photograph: Michael Freidin)

The Centre's Silver Jubilee. From right to left: Mayor Uri Amit, Betty Dubiner, President Chaim Herzog, Ora Herzog, David Pincus, Gerry Pincus and Marlene Post.
(Photograph: Michael Freidin)

The Centre's Silver Jubilee.
(Photograph: Michael Freidin)

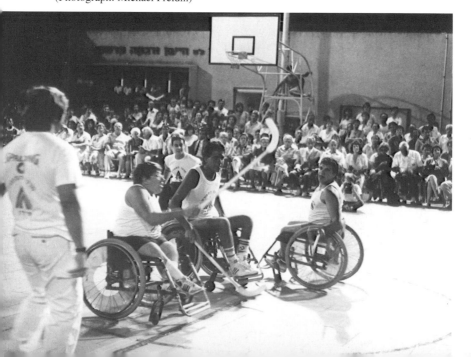

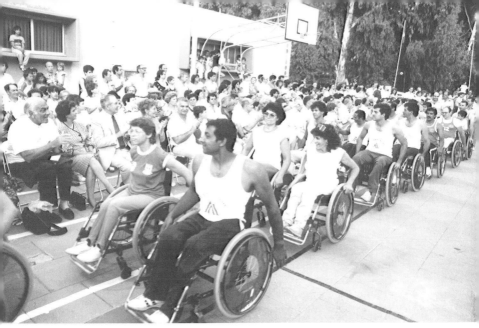

The Centre's Silver Jubilee.
(Photograph: Michael Freidin)

The Centre's Silver Jubilee.
(Photograph: Michael Freidin)

Tennis momentum – champion Baruch Hagai in action.
(Photograph: Michael Freidin)

Fencing develops courage and instinctive reaction.
(Photograph: Michael Freidin)

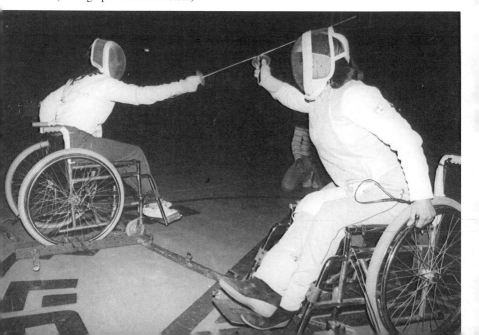

The opening of The Michael Simmons Disabled Children's Gymnasium. President Chaim Herzog thanking the Simmons Family for enabling the construction of the new facility. From right to left: President Herzog, Jan Cohen and Sarah Gold (daughters of Michael & Sheila Simmons).
(Photograph:Michael Freidin)

The opening ceremony of The Michael Simmons Disabled Children's Gymnasium: Ann Randall presenting a token to President Herzog on behalf of the Centre.
(Photograph: Michael Freidin)

Pope John Paul II speaking to Baruch Hagai while meeting the Israeli wheelchair basketball team during their visit to Rome for the Italian Open wheelchair basketball championships.

Mariel Arbutman, paralysed in both arms and both legs, playing table tennis.

(Photograph: Michael Freidin)

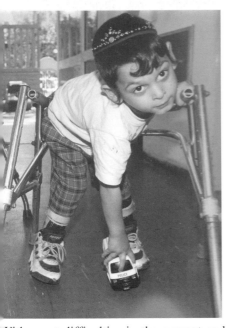

With great difficulties in the present and great hopes for the future.
(Photograph: Chloe Sherman, Oakland, CA)

Basketball star Michael Jordan, meeting Baruch Hagai. Standing at the right: Mickey Gitlitz, Jordan's former manager.

In the heat of the game – excellence has its price.

Nate Shapiro, Vice President of the Centre's Midwest Friends Committee, and former president of the American Association for Ethiopian Jews, with his wife Randy, meeting disabled Israeli athlete Israela Tasma and her sister Miriam.
(Photograph: Michael Freidin)

Bruce Rosenzweig, former President of the Midwest Friends Committee, coaching ISCD athletes. From left to right: Israela Tasma, Inbal Sa'idi, Rinat Baruch.
(Photograph: Michael Freidin)

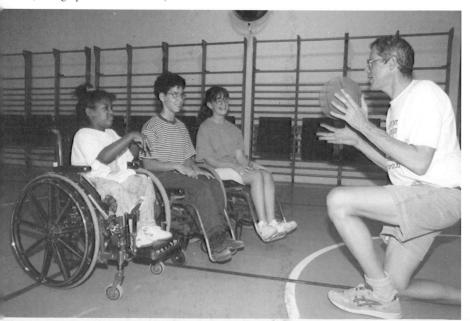

WITH ALL HIS HEART
AND MIGHT

Sam and Bella Spewack were the Centre's first
supporters from outside Israel. The plight of suffering
children moved them deeply. Others soon followed their
example. It is no coincidence that people who have
themselves experienced poverty and discrimination are
drawn to support charitable causes like the Centre.

The pogroms in Russia in 1882, and the outbreak of
the Bolshevik Revolution that followed, led the Jewish
shopkeepers and small tradesmen to flee the villages
of Eastern Europe. They sought refuge in Palestine,
America and Great Britain. The Jewish refugees hoped

to maintain their traditionally Jewish way of life, while being protected by their host countries against anti-Semitism. Michael Simmons and his brother John were the sons of such immigrants. Their father, Izzy, a tailor by trade, found work in London in a clothing workshop. Like many of the Jewish immigrants to Great Britain, he settled with his family in the poverty-stricken East End of London.

While Michael was attending kindergarten and primary school, he was sent to a private teacher for religious studies. His cheerful face soon became a familiar sight at the local synagogue and its choir. He also joined the Jewish youth club in nearby Ilford, and took part in Hasidic dancing and Hebrew classes. Curly-haired Michael, with his natural intelligence, was a typical Jewish youngster.

Curiosity led him to venture outside his own neighbourhood. He saw children playing football in one of the yards, and joined the game. He became very good at scoring goals. One day, as he was about to go into the yard, two burly hooligans barred his way. They didn't like the way he was dressed – which looked very foreign to them. They stood in his path. One of them said: "Get out of here, you dirty Jew!" Simmons furiously struck the boy who had insulted him. The two louts, who were surprised at his fury, quickly ran away. This was his first practical lesson on the problems of being a Jew.

Michael Simmons's father opened a small shop for clothing repairs. His mother, Rebecca, delivered the garments to the clients' homes. Twelve-year-old Michael used to baby-sit after school hours to bring home a little more money. He began to think about having a business of his own. His father, who respected his desire, said: "You should be a tailor Michael. A tailor! With a trade like that, you will always be able to make a living". Michael became an apprentice tailor under his father's supervision. But the war soon brought everything to a halt. London became a major bombing target for the Nazi Luftwaffe. Schools were closed, and the government began evacuating people from London. The Simmons family moved to a village in Cornwall, in the south-western corner of Great Britain. They opened a small workshop there for clothing repairs and, as Michael's father had said, were able to make a modest living for the family.

When the family returned to the East End at war's end, Michael was stunned by the devastation caused by the Nazi bombing. He noticed around him blind people, amputees and paraplegics, confined to wheelchairs. One day he came upon a young amputee slowly making his way along the road. The man had lost a leg as well as his sight. Michael had a shilling in his pocket – a large amount of money for him in those days. With tears in his eyes, he went up to the amputee, slipped the shilling into his pocket, and ran off. He was embarrassed, but also proud of what he had done.

His father rented a small shop in London's East End, and the tailoring activities continued. After a few years, Simmons was conscripted into the army. His parents were less than happy about this development. They were concerned about the bad influences in such a non-Jewish environment. Simmons himself saw things differently. From the East End, it was difficult for him to find his way out into the big city of London. From the army – he hoped he would be able to do so more easily.

One morning, as he went into the barracks' washroom, he heard a shout in his direction: "Jews use the washroom last!"

He then realized that even now, wearing His Majesty's uniform, he was still getting racist comments thrown at him. Michael's reaction was immediate. He vigorously punched the offending soldier in the face, and shoved him towards the washbasins. He caught hold of the soldier's hair, clenched his fist in front of his eyes, and demanded an apology.

The soldier sought his friends' assistance but, since none was forthcoming, mumbled: "I ... didn't mean ..."

"Apologise" Simmons insisted, "... before I stick your head in the basin." The soldiers around them looked on with a degree of admiration. The British have a great respect for courage.

"I apologise," the lad murmured quietly.

Simmons released him. The two remained standing, facing each other. The other soldiers in the washroom slapped them both on the back, as if to say – this incident is over. Let's forget about it. Thus, the second lesson that Simmons learned was that, although it's difficult to be a Jew, some courage and strength go a long way.

After his army discharge in 1954, Michael Simmons went back to working with his father. His proposals for expansion and changes in the shop fell on deaf ears. He realized that he would have to seek his future elsewhere. The clothes shops in London beckoned, some of them with "Help Wanted" signs. He found a position as a shop salesman. The owner quickly realized his potential as a salesman, and promoted him to Manager. However, after two years of hard work as an employee, resourceful Simmons understood that the rewards would be greater if he was self-employed. Together with a young London fashion designer, he opened a shop in London's Carnaby Street. The new business was a success, but it was a partnership. Now he wanted something that was his alone.

He bought a small, second-hand truck from army surplus supplies, and converted it into a sort of miniature, mobile boutique. He crammed hundreds of women's garments, purchased from the London clothing manufacturers, into the truck. He then took his mobile boutique to the retail clothing stores in London's suburbs and countryside, and easily sold the merchandise. It wasn't long before he needed more trucks. One morning, Simmons woke up and came to the conclusion that he would be better off producing his own merchandise. He believed that he could do it better, produce more attractive garments and, most importantly, do it more quickly and with less expense. He felt that he was able to sense the mood of the market just as well as anybody else. At this moment of enlightenment, he decided on a name for his fashion outlet – "Shelana". In his Yiddish Hebrew, this sounded like the Hebrew word "shelanu" ("our"), and also reminded him of his sweetheart, Sheila, who was later to become his wife. His new designs were well received by the market. Simmons expanded his fleet of mobile boutiques and, in early 1967, rented a shop with a large display window in the heart of London's fashion district. His next target was to conquer central London.

One day, an attractive girl in a revealing French-inspired miniskirt caught his eye. When he enquired in the London boutiques as to the cost of such an outfit, he was astonished at the high price they were commanding. It was then that he decided that he would manufacture miniskirts, at a price that almost every young woman could afford. His low-cost skirts soon reached the shops and the young girls of London snapped them up. His breakthrough on the fashion scene was covered in the London press. Simmons was selling twenty thousand miniskirts a week – which was as many as he could manufacture.

Despite his energetic business operations, Simmons never forgot the war wounded, and he started donating funds to the Jewish blind in London. With the Six-Day War, his Jewish identity was strengthened even more. The story of the war seemed to reflect his own life experiences. A nation, which appeared weak, suddenly stiffens its backbone and strikes a blow in the face of the burly hooligans threatening from all sides. Immediately after the Six-Day War, he came to Israel for a one-month stay, together with his wife Sheila, his daughters Jan and Sarah, and his friends of many years, Ann & Ken Randall. Simmons's business acumen had brought him money and power. Now, he used his success to benefit Israel. He began supporting the Israel war effort through the Joint Israel Appeal. When he heard about the Israeli disabled sports team's participation in the Stoke Mandeville Games, he invited the team to his showroom for a lavish cocktail party. He then joined the British Friends of Israel War Disabled, and served as the organization's Honorary Vice-President. Simmons liked the fact that the BFIWD invited groups of disabled Israeli ex-servicemen to visit Great Britain. He felt that meeting with the warm Anglo-Jewish community would accelerate their rehabilitation. This cause was very important to him.

Simmons became a frequent visitor to Israel in those days. During one of these visits he even met Dr. Henry Kissinger, former U.S. Secretary of State, who – like Michael – was a football enthusiast. In the late 1970s, Simmons bought a home in Herzliya, to gain a foothold in Israel, and was introduced to the Centre. He became a regular visitor, and spent many hours watching the disabled children at their activities. The Centre touched his heart deeply. He was impressed by the spirit and enthusiasm of these young disabled athletes. Simmons also had a high regard for the many hours of training put in by the disabled athletes. It was this atmosphere of determination that conquered his heart. He resolved that he would help this small facility to grow. In order to achieve this objective, Simmons persuaded his affluent friends in London and all over the world to join the circles of the Centre's supporters. In recognition of his great involvement and support, the Centre elected him as its honorary president.

One cold and rainy winter's day, accompanied by his friend Howard Sinclair, Simmons came to the ramshackle basketball gymnasium with its leaky roof. Coach Reuven Heller was holding a training session and shouting instructions to his trainees, who were milling around in their wheelchairs. They didn't allow the cold or the rain, which was seeping in through the roof, to dampen their spirits. Simmons was impressed by this spectacle, and enthusiastically told the Centre's Director: "We're going to put up a new gymnasium for these wonderful athletes!" His face beamed with joy as if he could already see the finished project in front of his eyes.

"It'll cost money, Michael, a lot of money."

"There are Jews in the world," answered Simmons, "Jews will always help. I will be the first one to give."

One year later, a spacious new gymnasium with a wheelchair basketball court was offering its services to the disabled. The use of prefabricated sections of fire-resistant wood had facilitated the swift construction of the building. The better conditions in the new gymnasium gave fresh energies to the disabled basketball players. The number of teams playing at the Centre grew, and results in the international sports arena improved.

Simmons now enthusiastically announced that, together with his colleagues in London, he would donate funds for the construction of an additional gymnasium. This building would be designed by a world class architect specifically for the use of disabled children. It would be constructed from the very best materials. Simmons's intention was that every nook and cranny of this new building would reflect respect and love for the children who would be training in it. He believed that this would positively affect the children's spirit and self-esteem.

At the end of 1989, after two years of planning and construction, the Michael Simmons and the J.I.A. Fashion & Menswear Committee Disabled Children's Gymnasium was officially opened. The gymnasium was equipped for the physical needs of disabled children. It even included basketball hoops that could be lowered or raised according to the age of the children and their abilities. Then President of Israel, Chaim Herzog, attended the opening ceremony. Michael Simmons was unfortunately unable to be present for personal reasons, but his daughters, Jan Cohen and Sarah Gold, and his friends, Ann & Ken Randall, represented him. A few months after the inauguration ceremony, Simmons's expectations were again realized. The impressive building, designed by Architect Moshe Levy, was selected by the Israeli architects' journal as the most impressive public building to be built in Israel in 1989.

Simmons's devotion to the Centre's work increased over the years. In the 1990s, his business activities expanded to real estate. At the same time, his social contacts with important public figures in London's Jewish business community also increased, and he began recruiting some of them as new supporters of the Centre. A special response came from philanthropists Dame Gail and Gerald Ronson. Along with their support of national, social, educational and Jewish causes, the Ronsons also promote and support Jewish security and self-defence against anti-Semitic attacks in Jewish educational facilities and synagogues in Great Britain. With his great charisma and conquering charm, Simmons convinced the Ronsons to also fund the security arrangements for the 4-acre Centre in Ramat Gan.

Simmons doesn't stop for a moment in his efforts to recruit new donors and new friends for this cause – which is so important to him. He has been doing it for over four decades, with all his heart and all his might.

THEY ARE MY CHILDREN

David Pincus is well known in the United States as an important art collector and prominent menswear manufacturer. Married to Gerry, he is father to two daughters and a son. However, this portrayal is only one side of the coin, showing a small facet of the life of this benevolent and complex man. David Pincus's parents, Nathan and Pauline, immigrated to the United States in 1906 from notoriously anti-Semitic Russia. A few years later, the traditionally religious family began manufacturing menswear – later becoming one of the largest menswear manufacturers in the United States.

Pincus was born in America, where his schoolmates respected his physical strength and his deeply rooted sense of justice. He became an impressive, tall young man with a deep voice, radiating charisma. He excelled in his studies at Penn State University, where he was also enthusiastically active in track and field events. His excellent achievements in throwing the discus led him to the 1948 U.S. Olympic Team.

Pincus enjoyed life and avidly admired culture and the arts. However, the war cut his studies short. He enlisted in the Merchant Marines, and was shipped off to the Pacific. The tall, robust young seaman never shirked hard work, and was always ready to volunteer for difficult missions. As a Jew, he hoped to be able to fight against Nazi Germany, but found himself stationed on the Pacific front. Later, in Europe, as a lieutenant, he carried out missions for the U.S. services and also for the CARE organization. He had no time now for the sports activities that he so enjoyed. At this time, David's older brother, Irwin Nat Pincus, was serving as a colonel in the Intelligence Corps of the U.S. Air Force, which was bombing Nazi Germany.

After his discharge from the Navy, Pincus completed his degree at Penn State University. The victory over Germany had made him aware of the atrocities inflicted on the Jews. His awareness of his own Jewish heritage was forcefully awakened. No one had protected the Jewish people during the Holocaust, and they had been helpless – an image that now reflected on Jewish survivors the world over. He believed that the way to change this image was to increase Jewish involvement in sports activities. However, most of his parents' generation, who had emigrated from Europe, believed that studying and working hard to develop a career were the most important objectives for young people. Sports and physical activity held no importance for them. This situation motivated Pincus to join the U.S. Committee/ Sports for Israel.

At that time, the newly-born State of Israel opened its gates to welcome the survivors of the European Holocaust. No other nation in the world had done this. Contacts between Israel and the Jewish Diaspora were stronger than ever. Jews the world over felt that it was their duty to strengthen the fledgling state. Pincus invested great efforts into promoting the growth of the U.S. Committee/ Sports for Israel (later: Maccabi USA/ Sports for Israel) and its activities in Israel. He also served for many years as vice president of this organization, being active in the organization of the quadrennial Maccabiah Games in Israel.

Pincus's commitment to the Jewish people did not lessen his sensitivity to the suffering of others. The human misery in the slum areas of his native Philadelphia motivated him to bring food to the hungry, wretched and homeless there. He wanted to do everything by himself, to make sure that things were done properly. In the hard, cold days of Philadelphia's winter, he met dozens of street dwellers. He distributed in Philadelphia huge baskets, with signs asking the residents to fill them with old clothes and blankets. After only a few days, Pincus had collected hundreds of blankets and coats, which he delivered to those in need.

Driven by a deep feeling of social responsibility, he often visited hospitals caring for terminal cancer victims. Struggling to keep the tears from his eyes, he would pass between the beds of patients who were barely able to breathe. He spoon-fed those about to die, who had already lost any appetite or desire to live. He embraced them – as if to transfer to himself some of their suffering. He increased his activities to help the local homeless and hungry. He did so with great conviction, feeling that he was chosen for this mission, undertaken by the Jewish people, to bring salvation to the world's suffering.

In 1980, Pincus met the Centre's basketball team, which was visiting the United States for friendly games with American wheelchair basketball teams. Alan Sherman from Washington, one of the U.S. Committee/Sports for Israel leaders, and later Chairman of the International Jewish Sports Hall of Fame, organized the series of games together with a young, Jewish leader, Marlene Post. Post, a nurse by profession, was married to the well-known Jewish physician, Dr. Robert Post. Among other positions she holds today, Post is Past National President of Hadassah USA, and a former President of Hadassah International.

One of the highlights of the basketball team's visit was an exhibition game they played, in front of 20,000 spectators, during the interval of an NBA game between the Philadelphia 76ers and the Washington Bullets (later, the Washington Wizards). This event was initiated by the Washington Bullets' owner, Abe Pollin, a generous and warm-hearted Washington Jew. Pollin also organized a lavish dinner at the stadium restaurant for the Israeli team and some fifty of his Washington friends – who made considerable donations to support the Centre's rehabilitative sports activities.

Pincus came to watch several wheelchair basketball games of the visiting Israeli team. He had not expected to see such speed and movement. In those days, society regarded the disabled as being doomed to a sedentary life. These disabled sportsmen had become strong despite their physical disabilities, which reflected Pincus's ideal of turning the weak Jew into a strong one through sports.

This meeting motivated Pincus to visit the Centre. He was deeply moved by the sight of the disabled children. He was able to identify with this cause with every element of his being. His visits became more frequent. He joined the disabled children in their training sessions. At these times, he became a different person – like the children he trained with – full of the joys of life, shouting out with happiness at everything that was happening around him. After the training sessions, he would open his big bags and give the kids sweets, dolls and Snoopy watches. The kids loved their very special friend from America. Pincus became an admired and familiar figure to the disabled children. The emotional bonds he shared with these disabled kids filled his heart with satisfaction and joy.

From 1980 on, Pincus served as National President of Israel Sport Centre for the Disabled's U.S. Friends, and volunteered the use and services of his offices in New York and Philadelphia. Donations from the United States became a vital factor in the Centre's development, enabling improved intensive treatment possibilities for disabled children and adults alike.

During the first Gulf War, in 1991, when the Iraqi Scud missiles were raining down on Israel, and particularly on Ramat Gan where the ISCD is located, Pincus rushed to Israel. He felt that he was needed there. He wanted to be with his own people at a time when destruction threatened once again. Although a number of missiles fell close to the Centre, it did not cease its activities. Pincus established his headquarters at the ISCD, and sent out bulletins to his friends all over the world. He described the daily difficulties faced by the Israeli populace, and particularly the disabled, who were confined to their wheelchairs. He spent much of his time sealing rooms against possible gas attacks, and playing with the disabled, whose gas masks were slung over their shoulders.

A strong friendship developed between David Pincus and Nobel Prize-winning author and Holocaust survivor, Elie Wiesel, who established "The Elie Wiesel Foundation for Humanity". Wiesel and his wife Marion appreciated Pincus's aspirations and his ability, by personal example, to try to change the world. At the end of 1993, in the midst of a bloody sectarian war in Yugoslavia, Pincus and Wiesel tried to arouse the world's conscience, and save the victims of this brutal warfare. The two made several trips to the region, distributing food, clothing and medical supplies to the Bosnian war victims. Pincus became close to a family of Muslim refugees who had lost everything. He decided to take them to the United States. He rented a house in Philadelphia for the five-member family, made sure that they learned English, and that the children received university educations. He helped them to rebuild their lives in the land of refuge.

Pincus spent much of his time on errands of mercy for the survivors of natural catastrophes and genocide in Ethiopia, Somalia, Rwanda, Sudan, Mozambique, and in areas of drought, famine and other disasters in Asia and Africa. In the framework of these visits, he brought food and medical supplies to tens of thousands of starving individuals in drought-stricken areas, his main objective being to help the children. He joined forces with the International Rescue Committee and the CARE organization, of which he was a director. With the same devotion and generosity, Pincus supported the cultural and scientific institutions of his home state, becoming a patron of arts and culture in Philadelphia. The world of fine arts provided a measure of artistic relief for his spiritually gruelling involvement and patronage in places like the Sparrow Ministries, a hostel caring for HIV-positive infants and children in South Africa. Despite the costly life-prolonging drugs available, the kids at the Sparrow Ministries are doomed – but it won't be for want of food or love.

In spite of Pincus's involvement in diverse areas of the world, his devotion and love for Israel is never neglected. Nobel Prize laureate, and now President of Israel, Shimon Peres sent a message of greeting when David made the first donation to the Centre's Endowment Fund. Peres wrote about this special man's activities thus: "... Helping the disabled to rehabilitate themselves and to return to the circles of active and constructive life is of the highest moral importance to the Jewish people, which lost more than a third of its sons and daughters during World War II. The fact that a person like you is involved in so many Jewish and humanitarian causes, and your tireless efforts to save lives and bring relief from hunger, war and natural disasters, speaks of you as a very special human being".

The Gerry & David Pincus Fitness & Recreation Institute for the Disabled, a facility funded by David Pincus, was inaugurated in 2004. This new institute, which facilitates the provision of medical and therapeutic treatments for children with severe disabilities, had been very much needed. *Jerusalem Post* journalist, Josh Pollick, asked Pincus what motivated him to dedicate himself to this cause: "It's a very, very important part of my life.... I'm involved with many needy children in the world, but what makes these children really special to me is not only that they are Jewish, but that they are my children".

In that same year, 2004, Pincus closed the ninety-six-year-old family business, which had provided jobs for thousands of employees. Concluding this chapter of his life was excruciatingly difficult for him. He felt as if he were forcibly removing a vital part of his and his family's being. Pincus's primary raison-d'être now revolved around his efforts to put the world to rights. In the summer of 2006, during the Second Lebanon War, northern Israel was very heavily bombed. Tens of thousands were evacuated to the central and southern areas of the country. The evacuees who found themselves in the Tel Aviv area included dozens of severely disabled, for whom wheelchair-accessible accommodation was a necessity. The Centre turned some of its gymnasiums into provisional dormitories, and invited these disabled evacuees to stay for the duration of the war. Around forty seriously disabled and their families found safe refuge at the Centre for several weeks, receiving food, accommodation and medical care, together with sports and recreational activities. This special emergency project for the war victims was funded by Pincus and some of his friends in Philadelphia. Additional support for this endeavour was extended by the Jewish Federation of Metropolitan Chicago. Pincus rushed to Israel again at this stressed time. He again felt that Israel needed him. It was a spiritual and uplifting feeling. Towards the end of the war, he invited all the disabled evacuees and their families to a festive meal at the Centre, giving each disabled evacuee a handsome cheque – to make life a little easier on returning home. He did so because he felt that these were his children.

A HIVE OF ACTIVITY

The construction of an open-air swimming pool was made possible by a donation from U.S. friend Hyman Kaplan in the early 1960s. Only popular and inexpensive fields of sport were operated, which enabled the membership fees to be kept very low, so that disabled children from even the poorest families were able to pay the fees. Several Israeli organizations extended their support. The Garage Owners Association constructed a workshop for wheelchair repairs, as well as a wheelchair racing track. A modest table tennis gymnasium was added in 1966, thanks to U.S. donors Rebecca & Hyman Prashker, and a small weightlifting room was constructed in memory of Rickie Younish. A considerable variety of inexpensive sport activities was offered, allowing the disabled to choose the activities most suited to their natures and physical capabilities. Even the most severely disabled could now look forward to a more active life. As the range of sports activities increased, the facilities had to be expanded to absorb additional disabled children.

About two-thirds of the Centre's trainees were disabled children. A special, intensive programme, based on ball games, was operated for these kids. The programme grew as years went by, and became known as the Intensive Sports Empowerment Programme for Disabled Children with Devastating Injuries. Dr. Shayke Hutzler, an expert in rehabilitative sport, was nominated as director of this important programme, which enables disabled children to take part in sports – an activity denied them in the regular school framework. The Centre also intensified its activities for victims of Cerebral Palsy and other serious congenital problems and, later, for youngsters injured by Palestinian terrorism. The advances made in technology and medicine brought a sharp decline in the numbers of seriously disabled infants who died at birth. These children survive death, but have to live with the most severe and complex problems. In the 1990s, under Chairman Ory Slonim, "Variety Israel" began to pay the membership fees for the Centre's most needy disabled children.

***

The Six-Day War broke out in 1967, resulting in many new disabled war veterans. These new disabled were invited by the Centre to a large sports exhibition that presented the sports possibilities for the disabled. General Yitzhak Rabin, the IDF chief of staff during the Six-Day War, was guest of honour. Following the event, the Israel War Veterans' Organization requested that a special programme be operated at the Centre for war disabled, in which over two hundred disabled war veterans later took part. Two of these veterans became volunteers at the Centre. Maozia Segal was badly injured on the Northern Front in the Yom Kippur War. He was a triple amputee, having lost both legs and an arm, as well as one of his eyes. Thanks to his grit and strong determination, Maozia pulled through. He went on to chair a non-profit organization for the proper administration of public affairs, and, for several years, voluntarily coordinated the wheelchair basketball league in Israel. Maozia was also one of the founders of the "Simcha Charity", which followed the tradition of Simcha Holzberg, Israel Prize recipient, known in Israel as "father of the wounded soldiers". Maozia wrote about his war and rehabilitation experiences in his book, *To Begin at the Beginning.* He later also wrote a book about Simcha Holzberg, called *With Joy in the Heart.*

Micha Schuldiner was critically injured in all parts of his body, and also lost an eye in the same war while crossing the Suez Canal. His return to life was a true medical miracle. After a long recuperation, he volunteered his services to the Centre as a social counsellor to the disabled children, and became extremely popular with the kids. His warm and exuberant personality made him one of the Centre's most impressive emissaries, both in Israel and abroad, and his constructive involvement in the Centre's activities has continued for over three decades. The Centre's work to rehabilitate disabled war veterans created new contacts. One of the most outstanding of these was Ann Randall, who was born in Wales and came to London in her late teens. Through her work as a beautician, she made contacts in London's society. After her marriage to Jewish fashion businessman Ken Randall, Ann devoted her time to creating a warm home for her family, which soon included two sons. The Six-Day War awakened her Jewish side. After the war, she and Ken flew to Israel with close friends, Sheila and Michael Simmons. Ann became one of the most active volunteers for Israel's disabled war veterans. She was also involved in hosting the Israeli delegations to the Stoke Mandeville games. After Renee Berman stepped down as president of the British Friends of Israel War Disabled (BFIWD), Ann was elected to replace her. Ann also developed contacts with the Centre, and became involved in its development and expansion.

The Centre's over five hundred wheelchair basketball players were making outstanding achievements in the international sports arena. The small Bella & Sam Spewack basketball gym was no longer large enough to accommodate all those who wanted to play. The old building was demolished and, in 1981, a new basketball gymnasium was constructed in its place. This was made possible by the support of friends from Israel, the United States and the United Kingdom, as well as Israel's National Insurance Institute (NII). The new gym continued to bear the name of Bella & Sam Spewack. Only those who remembered the modest ceremony held in 1961 to inaugurate the original basketball gym could compare it with the opening ceremony for the large new facility. This time, the event was attended by President Itzhak Navon, Ramat Gan mayor, Dr. Israel Peled, Israel Sports Authority director, Uri Afek, and other public figures. Over a thousand guests attended the ceremony, which was covered by all the Israeli media.

The next goal, in the 1980s, was to construct an indoor hydrotherapy pool for the seriously disabled children. Funds for this project were raised among the Centre's traditional friends in the United States and the U.K. A generous bequest was also received from Switzerland, from the late Sonia & Marco Nadler. To cope with the great spurt of development, David Weinreb, a young disabled athlete and experienced engineer, was elected as honorary technical advisor to the Centre. Weinreb later became a senior director at Bank HaPoalim, and, then, a business entrepreneur.

As increasing numbers of disabled joined, new branches of sport were needed. In the late 1970s, ISCD friends Murray Goldman from Canada, Martin Boston from the U.K., and Dr. Ian Froman and Kollie Friedstein of the Israel Tennis Centre suggested that wheelchair tennis be played in Israel. A group of disabled youngsters began training under volunteer tennis coach Amnon Bar'am, using the Centre's basketball court. After about six months, the training sessions were transferred to the Israel Tennis Centre (ITC). Tennis was an adaptable game for the disabled, with great social merits. Ann Randall persuaded U.K. businessman Mike Gross, who had served as a volunteer with the Israeli Paratroopers Brigade, to contribute, together with his parents, to the construction of two tennis courts, conditional on matching contributions being raised in Israel. Several organizations rose to the challenge, including the NII, the Israel Sports Betting Association and the Sports Authority. Two tennis courts for the disabled were constructed and named in honour of Morena and Peter Gross, the parents of the primary donor. During the first year, over one hundred disabled children and fifty disabled adults took part in the tennis programme. By 1984, the number of disabled participants in the wheelchair tennis programmes included about a hundred children and a hundred and fifty adults, and the ITC in Ramat Hasharon adopted the Centre's tennis programme for disabled children. The young wheelchair tennis players from Israel reaped considerable success all over the world in international tournaments, including several World Cup gold medals. Their success was supported by the Alec & Eve Sherman Foundation and Peter & Morena Gross from the U.K., and Dr. Alec Lerner of Savyon, Israel. From 1985, the Centre began hosting the second largest international wheelchair tennis tournament of that time. The Centre's wheelchair tennis branch had a successful win at the 2008 Beijing Paralympics, when ISCD athletes Shraga Weinberg and Boaz Kramer were Paralympic silver medallists for Wheelchair Tennis Doubles. Together with them on the winners' podium stood also their committed coach Kobi Weiner.

The spacious basketball gymnasium was unsuitable for the special needs of disabled children, who felt lost in its seemingly endless space. This triggered the idea of building a smaller gymnasium, specially adapted and equipped for children. This concept captivated the mind of Michael Simmons. In co-operation with the J.I.A. Fashion & Menswear Committee in London, and its representative Michael Mohnblatt, Simmons met the cost of this new project, which was completed and inaugurated in 1989 in the presence of President Chaim Herzog and Michael's daughters, Jan Cohen and Sarah Gold, and bears Michael Simmons's name.

The large open-air swimming pool also required a thorough overhaul every few decades. A major donor was needed. Through the contacts of Eleanor and Otto Kahn from Los Angeles, the Milken Family Foundation was introduced to the Centre, and, from 1991, undertook to donate funds towards this project. Michael Milken grew up in a typical American Jewish home. His father, Bernard, was a victim of Polio, and was wheelchair-bound. Despite his physical limitations, Bernard Milken got on with his life as a certified accountant. The children drew inspiration from their father's courageous way of dealing with his disabilities. Michael was an excellent student at California's Berkeley University, and later at the Wharton Business School of the University of Pennsylvania. In 1982, Michael, together with his brother Lowell, founded the Milken Family Foundation. To this day, Lowell Milken continues to head this important foundation.

***

Throughout the long years of expansion and development from the 1980s on, Jewish philanthropist S. Daniel Abraham has extended his generous support also to the Centre. Ann Randall introduced Abraham to the Centre. A traditional Jew, Abraham generously supports charitable causes, education and welfare in Israel and the Diaspora. Since the 1980s, Abraham has also been working towards peace in the Middle East, making use of his considerable international contacts to mediate between the Arab states and Israel. In the framework of this private diplomacy, which he initiates and funds, Abraham has flown to many Arab states in the region, together with U.S. Congressman Wayne Owens. He has met the national leaders of the Middle East, including those of Israel, with a deep conviction that peace is possible. Abraham's peace mission became part of the Clinton Global Initiative. Abraham's recent book, *Peace is Possible*, describes the motives and efforts invested in this complicated task. When the Centre's disabled children take part in the annual Miami

World Championships for Disabled Children, they often drop in to visit their friend at his home in Palm Beach, Florida. Abraham welcomes them with open arms, usually accompanied by the director of his charity, Rabbi Joshua Lookstein. During the most recent visit, Abraham presented the children with an autographed copy of his book in recognition of their achievements.

***

In the late 1970s, Maccabi USA/ Sports for Israel (MUSA), under the presidency of legendary basketball coach Nat Holman, backed by Maccabi USA leaders, swimming coach Jack Abramson, David Pincus, Bob Spivak and Alan Sherman, recognized sports for the disabled as being an inseparable part of the Israeli sports movement and worthy of its support. An important step towards recognition came years later, with the inclusion of disabled Israeli athletes in the Israeli delegation to the Maccabiah. Aside from its financial assistance, MUSA traditionally brings the U.S. delegations to the Maccabiah Games to visit the Centre. Bob Spivak's activities as MUSA president during the 1980s–'90s brought great momentum to the organization's support of the Centre, which was continued by his successors, Mrs Toni Wortman and Ron Carner.

Considerable help came from a unique charitable foundation in Geneva, founded by a group of non-Jewish professionals. These caring Swiss individuals choose to remain anonymous. They named their organization the Emouna Foundation (Emouna, in Hebrew, means "Faith"), and undertook to extend constructive support to disabled all over the world, including Israel. The contact with Emouna's Swiss trustees, Dr. Raoul Lenz and Mark Panchaud, was initiated through Nathan Zolberg in 1990. The Emouna Foundation contributed towards several development projects, including the renovation of the judo and yoga room, the table tennis hall, the weightlifting room, the social and recreation room and the installation of a lift. The contact with Emouna continues in the new millennium, as reflected in the 2008 visit to the Centre of Dr. François Chappuis and Claude Delacrétaz. Another important friend in Switzerland is the Rosenrauch Foundation, which makes a generous annual donation to support the Centre's Intensive Sports Empowerment Programme for Disabled Children.

Time never stands still. The new millennium began, and with it came new difficulties arising from the intensive use of old, worn-out buildings and equipment. Growing numbers of children needing the Centre's services necessitated, once again, the renovation and expansion of existing facilities, and the construction of new ones. The first major project of the new millennium was the covering of the Centre's large, open-air swimming pool, which, until then, could only be used during the seven warm months of the year. In order to enable the year-round use of the pool, the Centre initiated a campaign to raise the funds necessary to construct a covering for the pool. Support came from:

the NII; Ilan Ben-Dov (in memory of his father, Shlomo Ben-Dov); The Archie Sherman Charitable Trust (U.K.), David Pincus (Philadelphia, PA); The Harry & Jeanette Weinberg Foundation (Owings Mills, MD); Abraham & Rose Luski (Charlotte, NC); Bruce Rosenzweig (Chicago, IL); Friends of ISCD (U.K.); Larry Rosenzweig & Cindy Wong (Chicago, IL); The Ted Arison Family Foundation (Israel); Isaac & Sonia Luski (Charlotte, NC); Shelton & Carol Gorelick (Charlotte, NC); William & Patricia Gorelick (Charlotte, NC), and others. A generous personal donation from David Pincus enabled the construction of a second floor over the pool's changing rooms, The Gerry & David Pincus Fitness & Recreation Institute for the Disabled

Once the large pool was covered, the next project was to overhaul and renovate the hydrotherapy pool, where the Centre's most severely disabled children are treated. The work on this project was made possible by a generous bequest from the estate of the late Edith Kane (U.K.), as well as funds from the Friends of ISCD (U.K.), Marilyn & Barry Rubenstein from New York, Supporters of Israel's Dependants (U.K.) and the Beracha Foundation (Israel). The pool had become seriously overcrowded and, once the renovation was completed, additional treatment rooms and changing areas needed to be constructed to enable increased numbers of disabled children to be treated. Donations for this additional project were received from Rose and Abraham Luski (Charlotte, NC) and their son David

and daughter-in-law Cathi Luski (New York); Mrs
Beatrice Mayer (Chicago, IL); The Harry and Jeanette
Weinberg Foundation (Owings Mills, MD); the NII;
and Kennedy Leigh Charitable Trust (U.K.).

***

The Israeli government covers less than one percent of
the Centre's annual operational budget. Ninety-nine
percent of the Centre's budget are raised through
donations from private donors, foundations,
corporations and organizations in Israel and abroad.
From 1980 on, the NII and the Israel Sports Betting
Association have made considerable donations towards
the construction and renovation of the Centre's facilities.

Ramat Gan's mayors, Abraham Krinitzi and Dr.
Israel Peled, created a tradition of helping the Centre's
development and construction campaigns. Zvi Bar,
mayor of Ramat Gan from 1989, eagerly continued and
expanded this tradition. For a large part of his life, Bar
served as an admired paratroops' commander. During
the Yom Kippur War, he courageously commanded the
brigade that pushed back the Syrian offensive. He also
served as commander of the Border Guard, reaching
the rank of major general. Bar did everything possible
to expedite construction and other permits required for
the Centre's various projects, and was a constant and
popular visitor at the Centre's sports events.

It is important to note that many outstanding Israeli
artistes and journalists have become involved in the

Centre's activities as volunteers and supporters. These include: sports commentator Israel Paz; economic journalist and fighter against corruption Arie Avneri; popular international singer and composer David Broza; and poet, author, and television personality Amos Ettinger. These special, caring individuals, and many more – too numerous to mention by name – have left their marks on the Centre's development.

The success and example of the Centre motivated the establishment of additional facilities all over Israel. In the Centre's footsteps, the Zahal Disabled Veterans Organization established three large sports, recreation and social centres, called Beit Halochem, in Jerusalem, Tel Aviv and Haifa, and ILAN – Israel Foundation for Handicapped Children founded the Rehabilitation & Sports Center ILAN Haifa. In addition to the above-mentioned organizations, the Israel Association of Community Centres adapted their sports facilities to be wheelchair-accessible, so that sports activities could take place in their many community centres all over Israel.

Set among eucalyptus trees by the Yarkon River, the Centre, which spreads over four acres, now resembles a pleasant village resort, with low slate-roofed buildings, dotted with grass and flower beds. The support of caring friends in Israel and abroad has shaped the Centre, which, since its establishment, has rehabilitated over 20,000 disabled children – mostly victims of the Polio epidemics.

Itzhak Perlman visiting the Centre. From right to left: Sharon Huderland,
David Jerbi, Itzhak Perlman and his father Chaim, and Micha Schuldiner.
(Photograph: Michael Freidin)

Itzhak Perlman in training. Standing behind him – Coach Reuven Heller.
(Photograph: Michael Freidin)

Former president of Maccabi USA/ Sports for Israel, Bob Spivak, visiting the Center.
(Photograph: Michael Freidin)

Prince Charles with Itzhak Kabdiel (standing second from the right), head of the Israeli delegation to the International Stoke Mandeville Games in 1988.

A presidential visit. Ezer Weizman greeting the young athletes.
(Photograph: Michael Freidin)

Paralympic weightlifting champion Shmuel Chaimovitch. To his right – Coach
Avraham Bruner.
(Photograph: Michael Freidin)

Israeli Chief Rabbi, Israel Meir Lau, at the Centre.
(Photograph: Michael Freidin)

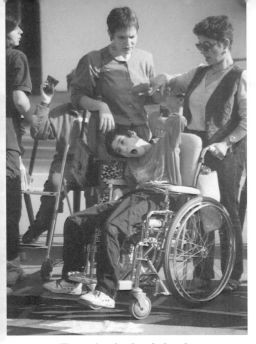

Every beginning is hard.
(Photograph: Michael Freidin)

The joy of the game.
(Photograph: Michael Freidin)

Israeli field event champion Geula Siri, in training.
(Photograph: Michael Freidin)

Former ISCD Chairman, Shmuel Hirschfeld, honouring Yoav Kreim.
(Photograph: Michael Freidin)

Lowell Milken, Chairman of the Milken Family Foundation, at the 1991
inauguration of the Milken Families open-air swimming pool.
(Photograph: Michael Freidin)

(Photograph: Michael Freidin)

Nobel Prize laureate Elie Wiesel with eleven-year-old athlete Boaz Kramer, campaigning for the Centre in New York.
(Photograph: Richard Lobell, Long Beach, NY)

Twenty years later: Boaz Kramer, Paralympic wheelchair tennis silver medallist, being congratulated by President Shimon Peres.

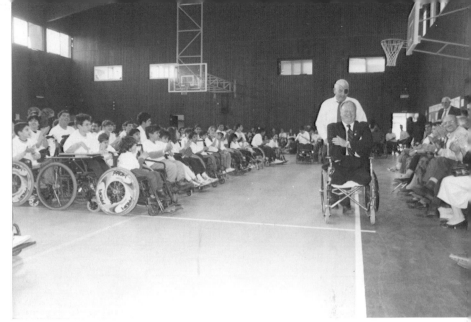

U.S. Senator Max Cleland from Atlanta (with Micha Schuldiner standing
behind) being welcomed at the Centre.
(Photograph: Michael Freidin)

Mayor Zvi Bar greeting Max
Cleland at the Centre.
(Photograph: Michael Freidin)

Max Cleland throwing the jump ball
for the basketball game.
(Photograph: Michael Freidin)

Campaigning in Chicago. Standing, from left to right: Midwest Friends Committee President Shelly Stillman, his wife Marlene, and son Jon Stillman. Seated in wheelchairs (left to right): Caroline Tabib, Idan Marash.

Time out – young athletes taking a break after a hard day of training. (Photograph: Michael Freidin)

The Centre's 40th anniversary – the wheelchair dancing troupe opens the event.
(Photograph: Michael Freidin)

Judo & Self-defence exhibition – Coach Danielle Ganapol (Black Belt Dan 5) and her son Yoel Ganapol.
(Photograph: Michael Freidin)

The inauguration ceremony of The Gerry & David Pincus Fitness & Recreation Institute for the Disabled. Standing, right to left: David Pincus, Minister Meir Sheetrit.
(Photograph: Michael Freidin)

Open-air activities all the year around.
(Photograph: Michael Freidin)

Guest of Honour Sir Jack Brabham (right) and U.K. Friends' Chairman Brian Harris (left) at the founding ceremony of the U.K. Friends of The Israel Sport Centre for the Disabled.
(Photograph: Tanya Harris, London)

Campaigning in the U.K. Vice-Chairman Irwyn Yentis (left) and ISCD Executive Director Jacob Ben-Arie. Seated, left to right: Mate Mazor, Shimi Skhayek.

Hon. Secretary Jane Jukes welcoming to London athlete Caroline Tabib, the Centre's awareness emissary.

David Weissman, President of ISCD's Florida Friends Committee, campaigning at a Jewish school to raise awareness and promote Bnei Mitzvah projects.

Good Wheel Bike Challenge. Riders from all over the world to benefit the disabled children in Israel.
(Photograph: Michael Freidin)

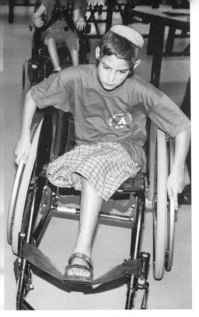

Terror victim Asael Shabo
at age 7, starting his long
journey to rehabilitation.

Terror victim Osher Tuito from bombed
Sderot at age 7, with National U.S.
Friends President David Pincus.
(Photograph: Michael Freidin)

Terror victim Eli Samira at age 15,
with Bruce Rosenzweig from Chicago standing behind.

Terror victim Elad Wassa at age 19,
with Coach Baruch Hagai.
(Photograph: Michael Freidin)

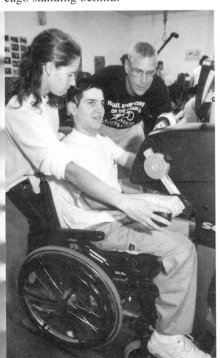

From the depths of misery and physical helplessness to the peak of sports achievement – Baruch Massami.
(Photograph: Michael Freidin)

Women's wheelchair basketball – an athletic experience and an important social motivator.
(Photograph: Michael Freidin)

The joy of speed. Racing wheelchairs and tricycles compensate for the disabled children's loss of mobility.
(Photograph: Michael Freidin)

An enthusiastic basketball novice.
(Photograph: Michael Freidin)

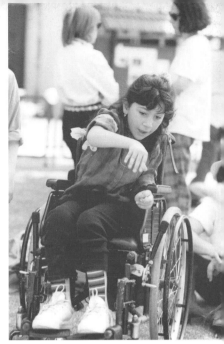

Hard beginnings.
(Photograph: Michael Freidin)

Popular music star David Broza giving his traditional volunteer concert.
(Photograph: Michael Freidin)

Caroline Tabib after winning a gold medal at the Miami World Championship for Disabled Children.

Mate Mazor – working harder and longer to achieve excellence.
(Photograph: Michael Freidin)

Prime Minister Ehud Olmert being welcomed at the Centre by Hon. Chairman Moshe Rashkes.
(Photograph: Michael Freidin)

THE BRITISH CONNECTION

Stoke Mandeville, where the first international wheelchair sports competitions were held, is quite close to London. While there, Israel's disabled athletes had the opportunity to meet some members of London's Jewish community, including Renee Berman, Rita & Walter Levy, Ann & Ken Randall, Rita & Gerald Levy, Michael Simmons, Cyril Stein and Avris & Leon Leboff. The idea of starting the Centre's first international friends' committee in London was conceived by Dov Reichmann and friends. The committee, named "Latzabarim", began awareness and fund-raising activities in the 1970s. It operated for almost a quarter of a century under Chairman Jack Feldman. Latzabarim ceased operations in the year 2000, and a new friends' committee was then founded under the leadership of lawyer Brian Harris.

Married to Shelley Katz, an author and screenwriter, Harris seems the typical, conservative British lawyer. Tall and dignified, with a cut-glass accent and understated British sense of humour, he epitomises the stereotype. However, he also drives a 1200 cc motorbike both on and off road in Europe, and also in various exotic locales, including India and Vietnam. His business career reflects his unconventional personality. He established the Flying Dentist Service in South Australia, represented the first British astronaut, the government of Uzbekistan, Aeroflot and Uzbekistan Airlines, and the first successful private charter airline in Moscow. He also successfully defended employees of a major tour company on charges of corporate manslaughter. He has acted in several white collar criminal cases in the U.K., together with lawyers in the United States and Australia.

Since participating in the Maccabiah Games as an enthusiastic fifteen-year-old, Brian Harris's emotional ties with Israel run deep. He felt a deep responsibility to help Israel's war disabled, and later served as national chairman of British Friends of Israel War Disabled (BFIWD), where he gained considerable public experience. This position also gave him a deep understanding of the problems encountered in the rehabilitation of the disabled, and the great rehabilitative merits of sport. After some eight years of successful leadership, Harris retired from BFIWD to become founder and chairman of the new U.K. Friends of Israel Sports Centre for the Disabled (FISCD), which – within a few years – became a thriving organization. The public announcement of the new central committee, in 2001, was made at a cocktail party held at the Royal Automobile Club, attended by many friends, volunteers and supporters. The Guest of Honour was Sir Jack Brabham, Formula One legend and five-time winner of the motor racing Grand Prix – a living example of courage and sport as a way of life. As charity begins at home, Brian quickly recruited the support of his brother John and sister-in-law Susan. Susan and John Harris became committed friends of the Centre. From the earliest days of the new committee, Harris worked in concert with Jane Jukes, a charming Canadian-born businesswoman living in London. Jane serves as the committee's active honorary secretary. Harris and Jukes, in the framework of their contacts with Israel, also began recruiting riders and participating in the recently begun ISCD Good Wheel Bike Challenge. This exciting annual fund-raising bike ride enables disabled and non-disabled to enjoy a four-day ride together, and provides an opportunity for the Centre's friends from all over the world to get to know one another better. Many new friendships are born during these rides.

Businessman and entrepreneur Irwyn Yentis, who played a major role in the establishment of the new committee, acts as vice chairman. With his impressive physique and personality, Irwyn Yentis still resembles the heavyweight boxer he was when he served in the British army. However, his physical appearance belies his benevolent personality. After his discharge as a captain from the British army, Yentis started out in London in the diamond business. Charity and Jewish solidarity always played an important part of his and his parents' lives, which led him to support Israel's wounded war veterans. After stepping down from an eight-year term as BFIWD chairman, Yentis sold up his diamond business in London, and retired with his wife, Hilda, to the seaside town of Bournemouth, on the southern coast of the U.K. Leisure-time activities were not what this energetic man needed. He went into the business world, and also set in motion the establishment of a friends' sub-committee in Bournemouth.

Through the initiatives of Harris and Jukes, appeals for support were sent to some of the large U.K. charities. Contacts were created with the Kennedy Leigh Charitable Trust, which adopted the Centre's Intensive Sports Empowerment Programme for Disabled Children for the year 2005, and contributed to the renovation of the hydrotherapy pool in 2008. Friendly advice was extended to the Centre by Michael Mohnblatt, a philanthropic management consultant, who – among other things – helped the Centre receive a three-year donation for the children's empowerment programme from the Sobell Foundation. The Archie

Sherman Charitable Trust, which joined the ISCD's supporters in 2006, helped fund the covering of the Centre's large swimming pool. Through Harris's good contacts, a generous bequest was received from the estate of the late Edith Kane, to be used towards the repairs and renovations of the hydrotherapy pool. The U.K. central committee's next initiative was to arrange visits of disabled children's teams to the U.K. – similar to those visiting the United States, and to organize fund-raising receptions for ISCD athletes coming to the U.K. to take part in international sports competitions. Warm contacts were created with important Jewish bodies, such as the Belsize Square Synagogue, under the leadership of Rabbi Rodney Mariner and his wife Sue. The Belsize Square Synagogue was founded in 1939 by Jews belonging to the Liberal Jewish Movement who had fled Nazi Germany. Since 1980, the community has been led by Rabbi Mariner, an outstanding educational figure with a charismatic personality and considerable influence beyond his own congregation. In recent years, the congregation has increased its support of Israel and organizes an annual benefit on Israel's Independence Day, the income of which is directed to Israeli charities. The Centre is fortunate to be one of these charities, and has sent teams of young disabled athletes to attend the event and meet the many guests. The Belsize Square Synagogue has become one of the Centre's major U.K. supporters. Good contacts were also created with the Queen's Club – probably London's most prestigious tennis club – and an annual fund-raising event has been held there in recent years. Considerable donations have been raised by FISCD to help the Centre purchase wheelchairs, and also towards the renovation of the Centre's thirty-year-old tennis courts, as well as ongoing repairs of additional facilities.

In 1965, Arthur Broza convinced The Helena Sebba Charitable Trust and The Samuel Sebba Charitable Trust to support the Centre's special pioneering programme for victims of Cerebral Palsy. Later, the Max & Helena Sebba Sports Awards and Tribute in Memory of Arthur & Sharona Broza were held each year, in order to present the rehabilitation of Cerebral Palsy victims. Jewish Child's Day, one of the U.K.'s well known Jewish charities, has been a traditional wheelchair donor for more than forty-five years. On the recommendation of Chicago-born friend Tal Litvin, the son of Dan Litvin and Kathy Sherman, Lehman Brothers Europe allocated funds towards the purchase of twenty-five much needed wheelchairs in 2006.

Another important long-standing supporter is the Lifeline4Kids charity, founded in the 1960s and headed by Roger Adelman, which has supported the Centre for over a decade. Its leadership, Chairman Roger Adelman and his wife Barbara, Jeffery & Suzie Bonn and Michael & Roberta Harris, keep a close eye on the developments funded by their charity. An additional important supporter is the Habad Orphan Aid Society, currently under the chairmanship of Ian Crooke, which has extended its support to the Centre for many years, through the involvement of Leon Leboff. Long-time friends of the Centre, Yad B'Yad Chairman Mordechai Hoch and his wife, Jane, also extend a helping hand whenever they can, as do the Supporters of Israel's Dependants charity and Mike Gross.

The Bournemouth sub-committee, established by Irwyn Yentis and chaired by Professor David Weitzman, has already organized several awareness and fund-raising events. It has made successful efforts to recruit major donors, such as Hilda & Samuel Marks, and their son David, who have made generous donations to the Centre, including the funds necessary to refurbish the Centre's cafeteria. Another important Bournemouth donor was Bertie Black, and his wife Doris, who made several donations to the Centre, including one to create the Social Services Room for the Disabled.

A second sub-committee was established in Nottingham, headed by Elaine & David Litman and Leni & Jo Gelblum. The Nottingham Friends always give a warm welcome to the ISCD's wheelchair tennis players, and cheer them on at the international tournaments held in Nottingham. In addition, they host the ISCD players at fund-raisers to benefit the Centre, raising funds for the purchase of wheelchairs.

THE MIDWEST STRONGHOLD

After completing his studies in Economics at the Illinois Institute of Technology, Coach Shaul Streifler integrated into Chicago's economic circles. He soon came into contact with the local Jewish businessmen, and regaled them with memories of his experiences in the Israeli army and at the Centre. Streifler understood that the plight of Israel's disabled children would find sympathetic ears in Chicago. Together with his friend, Dan Litvin, an entrepreneur and engineer who had served in the IDF's Golani Brigade, he made efforts to recruit funds for the Centre. The first Midwest donors were Devorah and Saul Sherman. In the mid-1970s, the first friends' committee on American soil was founded, chaired by Shaul Streifler. Dan Litvin served as treasurer; committee members included Devorah Sherman, Nate Shapiro, Sonny & Paula Stollman and Jed Malkin.

Streifler later suggested that a well-regarded local businessman be invited to serve as president of the Midwest Friends. Industrialist Sonny Stollman was chosen as president – a position he held for about six years until his untimely death. Businessman Jordan Kaiser was now elected to head the committee. He brought great energy and ambition to the task. Among the new members Kaiser recruited were: Larry & Lillian Goodman, Hezi Levy, Phil Cowan, Bernie Jaffee, Shelly Stillman, Milton & Gertrude Lambert, Al Winick, Ami & Miriam Koenig, and Karen May (now serving as State Representative for Illinois). Violinist Itzhak Perlman, who had trained at the Centre as a Polio-disabled child, volunteered his presence at a cocktail party organized by the committee at the Ravinia Green amphitheatre in Chicago during the summer concert season. This event was repeated a further three times during the 1980s and early '90s. Another musical fund-raising event was held with the help of the director of the Israel Philharmonic Orchestra, Avi Shoshani, who recruited the world renowned conductor Kurt Masur.

The annual visits of the Centre's disabled children's teams to the United States began to get under way. These teams were invited to Chicago to meet with donors.

During Kaiser's presidency, home fund-raising cocktail parties gathered great momentum. The main hosts of these events were: Devorah & Saul Sherman, Randy & Nate Shapiro (at their country club), Doris & Jordan Kaiser, Lillian & Larry Goodman, the Rosenzweig Family, Melissa & Ken Hoffman, Barbara & Dr. Don Hoffman, Dr. Susie & Dick Sigel, Milt Harris, and Maia & Howard Labow. At this time, Shelly Stillman initiated and funded a fund-raising Brunch, to which the team and supporters were invited. Many years have passed since this first Brunch, when less than a dozen donors participated. In recent years, the numbers attending the traditional annual Midwest Brunch have approached three hundred.

After Kaiser completed six years of presidency, Bruce Rosenzweig undertook the position of president. Rosenzweig was an all-round sportsman. He owned a yacht brokerage firm at the Chicago marina. As a devoted Zionist, his ties with Israel were already strong. His first encounter with the Centre was when the Israeli wheelchair basketball team played the Chicago Bulls. The Israeli team won, and Bruce and his father, Mo, were thrilled – especially Mo, who had immigrated to the United States from Poland in the late 1920s. In World War II, Mo Rosenzweig had joined the American Army and was serving on the Atlantic front when the Allies invaded Nazi Germany. For his combat merits in battle, he won a medal of honour. Together with his unit, he had entered the Nazi concentration camps, and witnessed the horrors. As a Yiddish-speaking Jew, it is

likely that he was one of the first to make contact with
the devastated Jewish survivors. The Holocaust shaped
Mo's spirit, and made him a very committed Jew. He
now felt that the Centre's work reflected the spirit of
modern-day reborn Israel, turning Jewish helplessness
into strength.

The Rosenzweig Family (Judy & Mo Rosenzweig,
and their children: Bruce, Larry, Sharon, David and
Michael) took the disabled children's swimming
championships under its wing, and made significant
contributions each year to sponsor this event. Bruce
Rosenzweig's commitment to Israel deepened as time
went on. He visited the Centre each year to attend the
annual event bearing his family's name as well as to
meet his Israeli friends. As an enthusiastic and
competitive bike rider, Bruce also initiated the Centre's
annual "Good Wheel" fund-raising bike challenge, the
first of which took place in 2006. Through much hard
work and exertion, the bike challenge has developed
into a significant fund- and awareness-raising event,
whose numbers increase each year.

During Bruce Rosenzweig's presidency, the Midwest
Friends succeeded in doubling the funds raised annually.
After six years as Midwest president, Rosenzweig
suggested stepping down, to enable another volunteer
to take his place. Shelly Stillman, a respected member
of Chicago's Jewish business community, was the next
to volunteer for the task. Stillman was also an active
supporter of the Jewish Federation of Metropolitan
Chicago, and the Israel Tennis Centre. The bond

between Marlene and Shelly Stillman and the Centre was particularly poignant, in view of the fact that their son, Jon, was born with severe disabilities. Stillman was a conscientious and devoted parent, endlessly boosting his son's spirit during the difficult hours of the rehabilitation process. His warm-heartedness and loyalty, and the confidence he instilled into his son, are typical of his nature and human values. His leadership of the Midwest Friends was a natural step. His son, Jon Stillman, and daughter-in-law, Phyllis, both of whom are disabled, also joined the Centre's circle of donors. They are a fine example of the part played by love and encouragement in the rehabilitation process of the disabled.

Shelly's endeavours to promote the annual Brunch required the active involvement of all the Midwest committee. Each member was responsible for selling tickets for the Brunch, and for its Silent Auction. Phil Cowan was chosen to head the Brunch Organizing Committee. Shelly now added another element to Midwest fund-raising endeavours, by organizing an annual Spring Theatre Event to benefit the Centre. An additional new fund-raising channel, a Texas Hold'em tournament, was initiated in 2007 by committee member Karen Nochimowski (married to Israeli businessman, Izhar [Izzy] Nochimowski). These events have added profitable new and social dimensions to the Midwest campaign, and recuited many new young friends.

Volunteers with high public merits lend momentum

to the Midwest committee's drive. One such example is Committee Vice President Nate Shapiro, a well known businessman and admired public figure in the American Jewish community. He is committed to public work on behalf of Israel and the Diaspora, and particularly Ethiopian Jewry. The old adage that you can't judge a book by its cover is most fitting for Shapiro. He looks like a mild-mannered Jewish businessman, athletic and tanned from his outdoor sports activities. His calmly pleasant public exterior reveals nothing of his long and stormy struggles to save the lives of Ethiopian Jewry and prevent another holocaust in a country oppressed, in the 1980s, by a bloody, totalitarian regime. Shapiro is one of the men referred to by President Clinton in his address, to the Raoul Wallenberg Award recipients, as "people who have devoted themselves to public service in the spirit of Raoul Wallenberg".

No less familiar in Chicago's business community are Saul and Devorah Sherman – and not just because of their philanthropic tradition. In his youth, Saul Sherman was a popular football star, playing with the famed Chicago Bears. His wife, Devorah, was a social activist, anonymously helping poor students fund their studies. She was active in promoting culture and arts, and worked also on behalf of disabled children, devoting much of her time to voluntary work in Chicago's rehabilitation centre. When the rehab centre became overcrowded, she organized summer camps for the disabled children in her then spacious family home on the outskirts of Chicago. Merely being members of the

Midwest Friends' committee wasn't enough for Devorah and Saul – they also became major donors. In recognition of the Shermans' many years of great support, the ISCD's annual basketball cup bears their name. In 2004, Devorah and Saul Sherman donated one million dollars for the Centre's Endowment Fund. The Shermans' example has paved the way for their children, John and Kathy, and also their grandchildren, Tal and Ariel Litvin, Ulysses and Chloe Sherman, to become involved friends of the Centre.

There are certain traits of human nature that reveal themselves with maturity. One such quality is the desire to help others. When this trait comes to realization, it can become one of the most gratifying sources of satisfaction. This characteristic is to be found in many of the Centre's friends. One special example is Beatrice (Buddy) Cummings Mayer, the daughter of the late Nathan Cummings – legendary philanthropist and art lover. Mayer followed in her father's philanthropic footsteps, and joined the Centre's supporters in the 1990s. The wide range of her social and benevolent activities reflects her background in social work, chemistry and the arts. Her business career was focused on managing the Sara Lee Corporation. Mayer serves as a trustee emeritus of the Nathan Cummings Foundation (which has made donations to the Centre); she is a board member of the Chicago Philharmonic, and of several institutions of education, museums and synagogues. In addition, she is a trustee of the Centre's Endowment Fund. When visiting the Centre, Mayer made friends with the disabled children. She maintains contacts with them, and keeps a maternal eye on their progress. Mayer is also involved in organizations for the disabled in Chicago, and particularly in "Access Living", an organization promoting accessibility for the disabled in public places.

Members of the Midwest Committee also recruited additional donors to benefit the Centre. Nate Shapiro's efforts resulted in the recruitment of major business figures, such as Alice & Robert Abt and Jon Mills. The home fund-raisers held in the 1980s and '90s had great potential, creating close contact between the supporters attending the event and the disabled children. Committed Chicago friends and benefactors, Lori Komisar & Morrie Silverman and Ken Lebovic, have recently returned to this heart-warming tradition. Morrie Silverman's involvement is unique. As an eleven-year-old child, he was seriously injured when he fell off a tree and, consequently, lost his right arm. In spite of this serious injury, he succeeded – thanks to his spirit and inner strength – in becoming a strong and successful businessman, and an ambitious golfer, who extends the one arm he has to help and strengthen others.

Chicago's Jewish community life revolves largely around the Jewish Federation of Metropolitan Chicago. The contacts between the Centre and the Jewish organizations are stronger in Chicago than anywhere else in the United States. These bonds, created during Lester Rosenberg's term as Federation chairman, were strengthened through Federation missions to the Centre during the first decade of the new millennium. Under Harvey Barnett's chairmanship, the ties grew even stronger and the Chicago Federation began supporting the Centre's work with disabled victims of Palestinian terror. Barnett also joined the Midwest Friends' Committee.

The support extended by the Midwest Friends in Chicago leaves indelible marks on the existence and development of the ISCD, enabling it to cope with the constantly growing numbers of disabled kids.

IN SEARCH OF FRIENDS

Prior to the 1980s, the Centre raised funds in the United States through the charitable foundation of P.E.F. Israel (Palestine) Endowment Funds in New York and, later, through the U.S. Committee Sports for Israel (to become Maccabi USA/ Sports for Israel [MUSA]). With the objective of creating independent fund-raising capabilities, a national friends' committee was established in New York. Businessman and philanthropist David Pincus was elected as national president, and Marlene Post as vice president. Lawyer Isaac Blachor was elected as honorary secretary, and also volunteered to register the committee as a legally recognized charity in the United States.

The committee's first project was to organize annual competitions with American teams for the Centre's wheelchair basketball team. These competitions, which continued throughout the 1980s and early '90s, attracted a considerable number of spectators – mainly from the Jewish communities of New York and Long Island. Many of these good Jews, through watching the games, got a first-hand glimpse of the rehabilitative value of sport for the disabled. The Israeli athletes were accommodated in the homes of Jewish hosts. As time went on, thanks to the friendly terms and considerable discount extended to the Centre by the Hotel Edison owners, Ulo Barad and Joseph Dunietz, the team began its long tradition of staying at the Hotel Edison in mid-town Manhattan. Marlene Post, who had good contacts both with the Jewish communities and also with the American rehabilitation scene, initiated the expansion of the games to additional U.S. cities: Boston, New Haven, Syracuse, Philadelphia, Baltimore, Washington, Las Vegas and Los Angeles.

The New York Friends' Committee also began organizing benefits for the Centre with performers, together with fund-raising cocktail receptions to host the disabled athletes. Singer and song-writer David Broza volunteered three performances in New York to benefit the Centre. Some years later, Broza also volunteered performances in Israel. The committee organized additional events, with the attendance of Elie Wiesel, Dr. Ruth Westheimer, and Israeli Consuls General in New York, Shmuel Sisso and Arye Mekel.

Since its earliest days, New York has been a hub of individualism. New York's large Jewish community has been successful in the business world, and its support was needed to advance the Centre's progress. Over the years, important New York donors were and continue to be recruited, including: Lorraine & Richard Abramson, Tom Waldeck, Michael & Judy Steinhardt, Hana & Kobi Alexander, Ilan Kaufthal, The Russell Berrie Foundation, Florence & Michael Edelstein, Marilyn & Barry Rubenstein, Madlyn & Leonard Abramson, Cathi & David Luski, Sylvia and Jerald Herman, and Claire Friedlander.

***

Considerable momentum was added to the New York endeavours when veteran New Yorker and Jewish leader Lenny Silberman got involved in the Centre's cause. Silberman, former vice president of Program Services and continental director of the JCC Maccabi Games, also served as athletic director at the Pittsburgh JCC (his hometown) and directed the Emma Kaufmann Camp. He was recently honoured by Maccabi USA/ Sports for Israel for his work and great dedication to this great organization. Silberman's smiling face is very familiar to the disabled kids at the Centre. His love for these children led him to organize the donation of a 40-foot container full of equipment for the ISCD's new Fitness Room. This energetic person overlooks nothing. He raises funds – even small amounts – from among his many friends and colleagues in the Jewish sports community. He knows that a large number of small donations accumulate to meaningful sums – so needed by the Centre.

***

One evening in the late 1990s, a group of young American Jews got together in New York after meeting the Centre's disabled children's team. These young professionals now felt an emotional need to lend a helping hand to the rehabilitation of Israel's young disabled. As relative youngsters themselves, they wanted to help in a different and more spirited way than their elders, as part of the Jewish tradition of social responsibility, while calling attention to the important role played by sports activities in the lives of the disabled. This led to the establishment of the Centre's Young Committee (YAD) in New York. With Marlene Post as mentor, the leading figures were Alicia Post (no relative), Tal Litvin, Seth & Celine Leeds and Matt Kamin. Additional young volunteers joined the committee as the years passed, including Justine Fisher. YAD organizes a traditional fund-raising cocktail reception, in one of Manhattan's clubs or art galleries, to welcome the Centre's disabled children's team on its annual visits to New York. The proceeds from these events are directed to the purchase of wheelchairs, a constant need of the disabled athletes. Some of the YAD members also accompany the disabled children to important sports events taking place in the New York area during their stay. As a result of these personal contacts, strong and long-lasting friendships have been created that continue to this day. In recent years, an energetic, new volunteer, Shraga Mekel, joined the Centre's fund-raising campaign in New York.

***

Two Holocaust survivors, the brothers Joe and Al Bukiet, reached the United States as penniless refugees. Their diligence, energies and resourcefulness led to their becoming successful and reputable developers in New Jersey. Their painful experiences in Europe strengthened their love for Israel. As years passed, they made contributions to the United Jewish Appeal (UJA), the Jewish National Fund (JNF) and Yad Vashem.

They also identified with the Centre's objectives and decided that New Jersey, too, could contribute to the rehabilitation of disabled children in Israel. Under their leadership, the first New Jersey Friends' Committee was established. The founding members included Cheri & Arnon Deshe, Beth & Dr. Edward Julie, Karen & Michael Bukiet and Annette & Mark Taffet. The methods of fund-raising were similar to those used in Chicago and New York – receptions in private homes or offices to welcome the Centre's disabled children's team on its annual visits. The brothers Joe and Al Bukiet organized the first New Jersey cocktail reception in the offices of their Bukiet Building & Management Co., in

Clifton, New Jersey in 2002.

Other committee members continued the brothers' tradition, and receptions were held several times in the Wayne home of Beth & Dr. Edward Julie, and also in the Franklin Lakes home of Karen & Michael Bukiet, and the Wayne home of Annette & Mark Taffet. These annual benefits continued, and other towns in New Jersey joined the effort. One such benefit was in Livingston, where the involvement of Seth Leeds led to an event being held at the home of Dara & David Orbach. In Teaneck, Myron & Charlene Schulman hosted a fund-raising reception at their home. Schulman also organized a visit to the Frisch Yeshiva High School in Paramus, New Jersey, whose students generously supported the Centre.

SOUTHERN FRIENDSHIPS

Max Cleland was born in the town of Lithonia, not far from Atlanta, to Christian parents of Irish and Scottish origin. His parents were working class, and he received a good education based on biblical values and a love of his homeland. At high school, he was an outstanding sportsman, and dreamed of an athletic career in basketball. Thanks to his charismatic personality, his handsome looks and his athletic build, he was very popular. Cleland went on to study U.S. history. Even as a student, he began to be politically active on behalf of the Democratic Party. In 1966, Cleland enlisted in the U.S. armed forces. Army life held a great attraction for this young patriot. Before long, he became an officer.

The Vietnam War – which in those early days was presented as a battle for democracy, and something that would soon be over – appealed to his spirit. He volunteered to be sent to Vietnam.

While on a military sortie, Cleland's helicopter landed close to the front line. There was a massive explosion, and he was flung to the ground by a huge wave of heat. For a moment, he was blinded. His body seemed to turn to stone, and only his heart continued beating wildly. He glanced dazedly at his right arm. Disbelievingly, he saw only torn khaki tatters, stained with blood and shattered bones. His arm had vanished. With a sense of foreboding, the young captain bent forward towards his legs. Covered in blood and soot, he saw his legs on the ground, a little way away from the rest of his body. Only his lower body, which had been shielded by a flak jacket, remained whole – as was his head, which had been protected by a steel helmet. A thousand red-hot spikes sliced through him, and he lost consciousness. When he awoke in the hospital, Cleland saw a group of doctors surrounding him. His faith in God had never been stronger. He had never prayed for a miracle more than at this moment.

During the many long hours of surgery, the doctors tied off and bandaged his two legs above the knee, and also his right arm. On regaining consciousness, Cleland felt like a cumbersome mummy, wrapped in bandages and bound to a bed. He was feverish, choking and thirsty. Shadowy hours passed. His first question to the nurse at his side was to ask if both his legs had been amputated. When he heard her positive response, he dared ask no more. His eyes, which scanned the blood-soaked bandages covering his truncated arm, told him everything. After another ten days of agonizing pain, Cleland was transferred to another hospital in Vietnam and then flown back to the Walter Reed Army Medical Center in Washington. When Cleland first saw his parents after his injury, he was embarrassed. He had spoilt the body that his parents had created for him. His father sought to reassure him: "You look good, son", he murmured in an uncertain tone, with a smile on his face that ineffectually masked his shock.

After several months of rehabilitation, Cleland began visiting the town, in his wheelchair, where he would meet some of his university friends from the old days. The girls usually left quite quickly. This caused him great frustration. He came to realize that if he wanted to cast off the shackles of his terrible disabilities, he would have to make an effort to rehabilitate his appearance, and to return as much as possible to his pre-war persona. Although his short stumps had not yet healed completely, he pushed himself to the limits. He felt that his body was gradually becoming stronger as a result of his physiotherapy. He began taking part in sports activities. After a long series of training sessions, he learned how to float. He also began playing table tennis. Sport returned to him a modicum of self-confidence, together with a feeling of manly prowess. Seated in a wheelchair, Cleland also started playing basketball, the sport at which he had excelled before his injury. He gradually developed a method of holding the ball, using the one hand he now had.

Because his leg stumps were so short, using prostheses was an extremely painful experience. However, Cleland wasn't put off by the pain, constant bleeding or lack of success. His desire to stand again was the most important thing in his life. Cleland left hospital before the completion of his physiotherapy. He purchased a small apartment in Washington, began to drive a car, and continued learning how to use his prostheses at the hospital's outpatient clinic. At that same time, he got a job with the public research committee investigating the activities of the rehabilitation services for war disabled. There was no one more suited to this task. Despite the fact that his prostheses continually cut and abraded the ends of his stumps, making it agonisingly painful for him to work, he stubbornly refused to remove them. Smiling through his pain but impressive in his appearance, he began to meet his old friends again.

Taking into consideration his physical limitations, as well as his desire to have a hand in shaping the national destiny, he felt that political activity could be a suitable occupation. Cleland decided to run for State Senate with the help of his friends from the Democratic Party. During his election campaign, he went from one neighbourhood to another, meeting thousands of people from all over the State of Georgia. His integrity, rhetoric, and his background as a war hero (he received a Bronze Star for Meritorious Service and the Silver Star for

Gallantry in Action), gave him his victory. On the election trail, he met an inspiring individual campaigning for the governorship of the State of Georgia. The two became friends. The candidate's name was Jimmy Carter, who indeed became governor of Georgia and, later, president of the United States.

Cleland was twenty-eight when he was elected to the Georgia State Senate. He knew that his success could not rest on his past glories or on the sacrifices that he had made for his country. His future success would depend only on what he could offer his public. He worked sixteen hours a day. His prostheses, which ripped open the ends of his stumps, were a nightmare. Specialists and doctors advised him to abandon them and to use a wheelchair. Now that his self-confidence had returned, Cleland realized that this was the only solution that would allow him to live his life without constant pain. The wheelchair became an integral part of his persona. Four years later, Cleland campaigned again, and was re-elected to the Georgian Senate.

When Jimmy Carter became president, he nominated Max Cleland as general director of the War Veterans' Administration, as well as a member of the U.S. Government. From being rehabilitated, Cleland now became a rehabilitator. In this framework, he hosted an important visitor from Israel – Arieh Fink, who then headed the Israel Defence Ministry's Rehabilitation Division. Fink asked him to allow American rehab specialists to treat several Israeli bilateral-limb amputees who had been wounded in the Yom Kippur

War. Cleland responded favourably.

Cleland's next step was to run for the position of secretary of state for Georgia. He was elected to this position for three consecutive terms. Despite his busy life, he found time to write his autobiography, *Strong at the Broken Places*, describing his long journey to rehabilitation, and always found time to pray before every meal, to thank God for providing his daily bread.

Former Israeli Consul General Arye Mekel made the introductions between Cleland and the author of this book, who invited Max to visit the Centre. For Cleland, a visit to the Holy Land, where Christ had lived, was a visit touched with immense emotional significance. The Centre organized a special wheelchair sports exhibition in honour of this unique guest. When invited to speak, moved by what he had seen, Cleland said: "I don't think I've ever seen such a group of athletes, such a group of people, so full of courage, so full of determination, and so full of strength, as I've seen today. I think it's a tribute to you and to your country". During his visit to Israel, Cleland was also invited to meet then Prime Minister Yitzhak Rabin and Foreign Minister Shimon Peres – who later became president of the State of Israel. Before Max Cleland's election as democratic senator for the State of Georgia in 1996, he had agreed to accept the honorary presidency of the Centre's Atlanta Friends' Committee. He fulfilled this position with deep commitment, never missing a meeting with the ISCD's disabled children's teams on their visits to Atlanta.

However, Max Cleland was not the Centre's sole

friend in America's South. The Centre's cause was important also to a number of good Jews in Atlanta. In the 1990s, Cheryl Coco, then personal assistant to Arye Mekel, Israeli Consul General to the Southeast, undertook the organization of the Atlanta committee with great talent and personal charm. This friends' committee was comprised of people with a love of Israel, many of whom had a sports background. One of these was industrialist Larry Frank, a graduate of Vanderbilt University, who had been an outstanding athlete in his youth, and captained the famous Gator Bowl football team. This was an admirable achievement for any sportsman, but particularly so, at that time, for a Jewish sportsman in the southern United States. Frank later became active in Jewish organizations, taking a central role as a national chairman of the UJA, campaign chair for the Jewish Federation of Greater Atlanta and chair for Southeastern Region Israel Bonds.

Larry's wife, Lois, was just as active in Zionist and humanitarian causes. A graduate of Emory University and Atlanta University School of Social Work, she became active in the civil rights movement. Notwithstanding her human rights' activities, Lois Frank voluntarily undertook positions of leadership in the Jewish community, including national chairman of the Jewish Council for Public Affairs, as well as being active in the Conference of Presidents of Major American Jewish Organizations and the American Jewish Committee. With this illustrious public background, the Franks' involvement with the ISCD has had a great impact on the Centre's work in Atlanta. The Franks have four sons, one of whom – Adam – lives in Jerusalem with his wife, Lynne, and serves as a community rabbi.

It is no coincidence either that a person like Mike Leven joined the circle of Atlanta friends. Leven is one of the most experienced hoteliers in the United States. Born in Boston's Jewish neighbourhood, he aspired to be accepted to rabbinical school. Fate intervened, however, and brought him instead to the world of business. He has administered the Holiday Inn, Days Inn, Americana and Microtel chains. Despite his business involvements, Leven has never forgotten his debts to society. In the hotels he managed, he opened up employment opportunities for the disabled, elderly and homeless, and returned many hundreds of disabled to gainful employment. These activities strengthened his desire to work for the public good. He became one of the leading figures of Atlanta's Jewish community, serving as vice president of the Jewish Federation of Greater Atlanta, and general chairman of the State of Israel Bonds Committee in Atlanta. When Leven heard that a team of disabled children was visiting Atlanta, he invited the team to be his guests at one of his hotels – thus beginning a tradition of many years. Leven became vice chairman of the Marcus Foundation, and then CEO of the Georgia Aquarium. He currently serves, where his great expertise is most needed, as president and COO of the luxurious Venetian Las Vegas Hotel Casino. Married to Andrea, he has three sons.

In 2006, the Centre's traditional circle of friends in Atlanta was reinforced by the addition of several important public figures from Atlanta's Jewish community who identified with the ISCD's goals. These included Michael & Marcia Schwarz, son Herman and daughter-in-law Lori Kagan Schwarz, son Barry and daughter-in-law Francie Schwarz; Lynne & Howard Halpern, son Kirk and daughter in-law Lori Halpern; newspaper columnist Lewis Regenstein; Ceil & Mark Euster, Debra & Joseph Berger and others. The group was later joined by non-Jewish social activist Linda Dean.

Following the Olympic and Paralympic Games in Atlanta in 1996, public awareness of sports for the disabled increased. Important new friends, Abraham and Rose Luski from Charlotte in North Carolina, joined the Centre's circle of supporters. Abraham Luski was born in Havana, Cuba, and graduated from the University of Cuba with a degree in Political Science. He grew up in a traditional Jewish family, with Zionism flowing through his veins from birth. His high intellectual capabilities were matched only by his passion for art and culture. The Marxist atmosphere of Castro's Cuba was not the right environment for a person like him. His family moved to Miami in the early 1960s. Luski was an unusual figure in the rough world of the American South. He had a pleasant personality, with a soupçon of European culture – but it was difficult to earn a living from art and culture in Miami at that time. Fortunately, Luski had another important quality

– a head for business. This enabled him to make his mark on the business scene and later, in partnership with his brother Isaac, to head the Shamrock real estate company in Charlotte, North Carolina.

Luski is active in almost every public Jewish activity in Charlotte. One of the causes closest to his heart is the preservation of the Yiddish language. For the past three decades, he has organized, in the mountains of North Carolina, an annual seminar celebrating the Yiddish language. Abraham Luski also founded the Centre's Charlotte Friends' Committee, serving as its honorary president since first becoming acquainted with the Centre in 1996. His daughter, Batya (Berta) Straz, acts as his right hand. Together, they organize a successful annual fund-raising campaign on behalf of Israel's disabled children. The Luski-Gorelick Families are traditionally the largest Charlotte donors. Batya's brothers, David Luski, and his wife, Cathi, and also Rabbi Jacob Luski, and his wife, Joanne, have also become supporters and friends, as have Abraham Luski's sister Marcia and her husband, Daniel Kokiel.

Yet another major figure in America's South is Federal Judge, Dr. A. Jay Cristol, of Miami. Cristol was a U.S. pilot in the Korean War. His book; *The Liberty Incident*, defends Israel's innocent motives in the IDF's bombing of the Liberty, an American naval spy ship, during the Six-Day War. Cristol spent eighteen years as a naval aviator, and twenty in the Navy's Judge Advocate General Corps. He retired as a captain in the U.S. Navy Reserve and lives in Miami with his wife,

Elly. His support for the Centre began in the 1980s, and remains unflagging to this day.

The first fund-raising initiatives in Florida were based on the personal contacts of the Centre's director with former Israelis now living in Miami. One of these was Nick Morley, Florida's largest land developer at that time, who began supporting the Centre. Another donor was the Israeli film producer and businessman Alex Hacohen, who also recruited Ted Arison, with whom he had served in the British army. Arison's support transferred with him back to Israel (and even increased with the later involvement of his daughter, Shari Arison). However, these donations from Florida were sporadic, and did not really get off the ground until David Weissman entered the picture.

Since 2002, a new friends' committee in Florida, launched and presided over by David Weissman, has steadily been gaining support. Weissman is a businessman and developer, and a long-time leader of Maccabi USA/ Sports for Israel. He has made many visits to the Centre in this framework. In recognition of his great involvement in promoting Jewish sport – and especially softball – Weissman was also inducted into the Israel Softball Association Hall of Fame. His great experience in promoting sport among Jewish youngsters in the United States, and his love for Israel, led him to organize in Florida a programme for Mitzvah projects to benefit the Centre. The Florida Friends' Committee was reinforced by additional new friends and supporters including Barry Gurland, Judi Gottlieb, Maggie & Paul

Fischer, Denise & Giora Israel and the B'nei Torah Congregation in Boca Raton.

Weissman's commitment and charm attracted additional important business and public figures in Florida to join him in his mission. One of these was banker and philanthropist, Commissioner Billy Joel of Aventura, and his wife Sandra. In recent years, Joel has been involved in the "Anchors Away" programme, which gives disabled children and youth in Florida the opportunity to learn to sail. The support of the Joel family for disabled children in Israel was therefore a natural step. An additional new friend in Florida at this time was Rubin Salant, a major supporter of Bar-Ilan University. This new wave of positive activity and commitment also attracted Daniel and Stephanie Gold. Daniel is an outstanding tennis player in the United States, and is also related to the Centre's good friend in London, Michael Simmons.

The warm ties with the Centre's friends in Miami are reinforced by the ISCD disabled children's team's annual participation in the Junior Orange Bowl Sports Ability Games (the Miami World Championships for Disabled Children & Youth). While in Florida, the children sometimes have the opportunity to visit Disney World in Orlando. Harris Rosen, the owner of the Quality Inn International Hotel in Orlando, warmly welcomes them, and generously provides accommodation for the Israeli team.

OLYMPIC GOLD

The first Paralympics took place in Rome, in 1960, with the participation of 400 disabled athletes and their escorts, from 23 countries. Israel's disabled athletes won 7 gold, 3 silver and 4 bronze medals.

At the 1964 Tokyo Paralympics, with 390 participants from 22 countries, the disabled Israeli athletes won 8 gold, 3 silver and 18 bronze medals.

In 1968, the Paralympics took place in Israel, with the participation of 1,200 athletes and escorts from 29 countries. The Israeli athletes won 22 gold medals at these Games, in addition to 20 silver and 24 bronze medals. Both the Israeli Men's and Women's Wheelchair Basketball teams won Olympic championships at these Games.

The 1972 Munich Paralympics hosted 1,400 participants from 44 countries. At these Games, the disabled Israeli athletes won 9 gold, 10 silver and 10 bronze medals. The Israeli Men's Wheelchair Basketball team took second place, and the Women's Basketball team took third place.

The 1976 Paralympics took place in Montreal, Canada. For the first time, amputees and sight-impaired disabled took part in the Games. The number of participants reached a high of 2,700 from 42 different countries. At this special Paralympics, Israeli disabled athletes won 40 gold medals, as well as 27 silver and 8 bronze medals. The Israeli Women's Wheelchair Basketball team took first place. The Disabled War Veteran's amputees' volleyball team also took first place. The Men's Basketball team won second place, and the Disabled War Veterans' sight-impaired goal ball team won third place. It was possible to send a large Israeli delegation to Canada thanks to a generous donation made by Murray Goldman, of Toronto, who sponsored the Israeli contingent.

Over 2,560 participants from 42 nations took part in the 1980 Paralympics held in Arnhem, Holland. Israeli athletes won 13 gold, 18 silver and 14 bronze medals. The Israeli Men's Wheelchair Basketball team won the Olympic championship. The amputees' volleyball team took first place, the Women's Wheelchair Basketball team took third place, and the sight-impaired goal ball team also took third place.

The 1984 Paralympics were divided between two

locations: the competitions for the paraplegics took place at Stoke Mandeville; the competitions for the other categories of disability took place at Long Island, in the United States.

At the Stoke Mandeville Games, with 2,300 participants from 45 countries, the Israeli athletes won 3 gold, 3 silver and 5 bronze medals. At the Long Island Games, where 1,700 athletes from 41 countries took part, disabled athletes from Israel took 2 gold, 7 silver and 6 bronze medals.

The 1988 Paralympics were held in South Korea. A record number of 4,200 participants from 62 nations took part in these Games. Israel's disabled athletes won 15 gold, 14 silver and 17 bronze medals. The relatively large Israeli team sent to far-away Seoul was made possible by the donation of Shaul Eisenberg, an international entrepreneur whose business interests were concentrated in the Far East.

The 1992 Barcelona Paralympics hosted 4,148 participants from 83 countries. The Israeli athletes won 2 gold, 4 silver and 5 bronze medals. The Israel Basketball Players Association (IBPA) helped raise the necessary funding to enable the wheelchair basketball team to travel to Spain. On the initiative of Lawyer (and past basketball star) Shmuel Zisman, chairman of the IBPA, a basketball competition between foreign players and local Israeli players was held at the Yad Eliyahu Arena in Tel Aviv, the proceeds of which helped cover the expenses of the Israeli wheelchair basketball team. This was a great gesture of solidarity on the part of the able-bodied basketball players in Israel towards their disabled colleagues. The Barcelona Paralympics also saw an improvement in the relationship with the International Paralympic Committee (IPC), in no small part due to the involvement of Marqués Juan Antonio Samaranch, who had been elected, in 1980, as president of the International Olympic Committee.

Atlanta hosted the 1996 Paralympics, with its 3,195 athletes and 1,717 delegation staff from 103 countries. The Israeli delegation, which included around 40 disabled athletes, won 4 silver and 5 bronze medals.

The Israeli contingent achieved better results in the 2000 Paralympics in Sydney, Australia. The Games hosted 6,943 participants, which included 3,824 athletes from 122 countries. The 34-member Israel delegation won 4 gold, 4 silver and 5 bronze medals.

Over 3,800 disabled athletes from 136 countries participated in the 2004 Athens Paralympics. The Israeli team of 24 disabled athletes won 4 gold medals, in addition to 4 silver and 5 bronze medals.

The 2008 Beijing Paralympics hosted more than 4,800 disabled athletes from 148 countries. Israeli athletes won 5 silver medals and 1 bronze medal. Israel's wheelchair basketball team, under Coach Arik Pinto, took sixth place.

EPILOGUE

Time has marched on since the Polio epidemic recalled at the outset of this book – for the world, for Israel, and for the Centre. What began as a humble rehabilitative facility to ease the plight of Polio victims and those injured in Israel's War of Independence, has turned into a highly developed and comprehensive endeavour to rehabilitate great numbers, disabled by congenital defects, diseases, accidents, war and terrorist activity. One thing, however, has not changed – the need to rehabilitate the disabled through sports activities and by strengthening their life skills, motivating them to return to circles of society and life.

This is a challenging mission – almost creating a new human being, determined to achieve the impossible – and sometimes even to do so. This objective holds a special appeal for people with social responsibility, who voluntarily join the Centre's efforts to shape the lives of those who have been so cruelly challenged by nature, war or human evil. All involved in this long and demanding endeavour are winners. All are doomed to glory at the final counting.

SALUTING THE VOLUNTEERS

U.K. NATIONAL COMMITTEE – LATZABARIM (Ceased operations in 2000)

Chairman: Jack Feldman; *Hon. Secretary:* Maureen Feldman; *Treasurer:* Ros Dunn; Brian Dunn, Ruth & Avi Eisenberg, Merryl & Leon Godfrey, Jane & Mordechai Hoch, Lily & Franklyn Kahn, Dahlia & Dov Reichman, Rita & Steven Wolfisz.

U.S. NATIONAL COMMITTEE

President: David N. Pincus; *Vice President:* Marlene Post; *Hon. Secretary:* Isaac Blachor; *Treasurer:* Marco Yeshoua; ***U.S. Members:*** Richard Abramson, David Bercuson, Barbara Glasband, Ellen Hershkin, Eleanor Kahn, Bruce Rosenzweig, Fred Schoenfeld, Nate Shapiro, Alan Sherman, Merry Slone, Robert E. Spivak,

Shaul Streifler, Tom Waldeck, Eitan Zur; *Israeli Members:* Israel Globus, Sharon Huderland, Moshe Rashkes.

FISCD U.K. – NEW NATIONAL COMMITTEE
Chairman: Brian B. Harris; *Vice Chairman:* Irwyn Yentis; *Hon. Secretary:* Jane C. Jukes; *Treasurer:* Jeremy S. Harris; Steven Davidson, Martin Gordon, Harold Newman, Saul Rachel.
Bournemouth Sub-committee: *Chairman:* David Weitzman; Bertie Black, Irwyn Yentis.
Nottingham Sub-committee: Jo & Leni Gelblum, Elaine & David Litman.

MIDWEST COMMITTEES
President: Shelly Stillman; *Vice President:* Phil Cowan, Nate Shapiro.
Executive Committee: Marilyn & Shelly Banks, Harvey Barnett, Arleen Cowan, Courtney & Richard Fahn, Stewart Flink, Irwin Friedman, Milt Harris, Barbara & Donald Hoffman, Ken Hoffman, Paul Hofman, Ken Lebovic, Dan Litvin, Phyllis Mitchell, Sheila & James Nerad, Karen Nochimowski, Richard Price, Bruce Rosenzweig, Susie Sigel, Abigail Sivan, Phyllis & Jon Stillman, Shaul Streifler.
Advisory Committee: Bruce Bachmann, Sam Borek, Melissa Hoffman, Ami Koenig, Elaine & Larry Ordower, Linda Price, J.B. Pritzker, Lester Rosenberg, Judy Rosenzweig, Renee & Elliot Roth, Al Winick.

Texas Hold'em Tournament Committee: Igor Elkin,
Courtney Fahn, Richard Fahn, Ken Lebovic, Stuart
Nitzkin, Karen Nochimowski, David Port, Andrew
Rintels, Brian Rubin, Gary Siegel, Scott Solomon,
Sergey Taitler.
Midwest Coordinator: Cece Lobin.

**NEW YORK COMMITTEE (Ceased operations in
1995)**
President: Richard Abramson; Lorraine Abramson,
Renee Albert, Barbara Chipurnoi, Paul Eisenberg,
Barbara Glasband, Ellen Hershkin, Gitta Jabotinsky,
Paul Kaye, Judge Samuel Levine, Blanche Narby, Paula
Oreck, Marlene Post, Merry Slone, Tom Waldeck, Gerry
Webber, Marco Yeshoua, Theda Zuckerman, Eitan Zur.

NEW YORK – YOUNG COMMITTEE (YAD)
Jonathan Ellman, Jonathan Ferman, Justine Fisher, Matt
Kamin, Bradley Karp, Celine & Seth Leeds, Dana &
Tal Litvin, Paley Munn, Alicia Post.

ATLANTA COMMITTEE
President: Max Cleland; *Hon. Secretary:* Linda Dean;
Debra & Joseph Berger, Cheryl Coco, Ceil & Mark
Euster, Lois & Larry Frank, Beverly Greenwald, Lori
& Kirk Halpern, Lynne & Howard Halpern, Mike
Leven, Erin & Trey Ragsdale, Lewis Regenstein,

Marcia & Michael Schwarz, Lori Kagan Schwarz & Herman Schwarz, Francie & Barry Schwarz.

CHARLOTTE COMMITTEE
President: Abraham Luski; *Hon. Secretary:* Batya Straz; Gloria & Harry Lerner, Marcelle & Dan Peck, Lori & Eric Sklut.

NEW JERSEY COMMITTEE
Al Bukiet, Joe Bukiet, Karen & Michael Bukiet, Cheri Deshe, Ellen & Dr. Joel Jacowitz, Beth & Dr. Ed Julie, Myron Schulman, Annette & Mark Taffet, Nira & Larry Traster.

ISRAEL SPORT CENTRE FOR THE DISABLED BOARD OF DIRECTORS
Hon. President: Michael Simmons; *Hon. Chairman:* Moshe Rashkes; *Executive Director:* Jacob Ben-Arie; Miri Ben-Yehoshua, Amihud Dvir, Nathan Gurski, Baruch Hagai, Uri Harlap, Shmuel Hirschfeld, Mordechai Huderland, Sharon Huderland, Amnon Inbar, Itzhak Kabdiel, Chana Laor, Ilan Lusky, Arieh Pinto, Ehud Rassabi, Efraim Raz, Yoel Shafran, Tamar Strauss, Shaul Sviri, David Weinreb, Amnon Weiss, Shimon Zurieli.

Index